Changing Our Minds

Changing Our Minds

Feminist Transformations of Knowledge

Edited by
Susan Hardy Aiken
Karen Anderson
Myra Dinnerstein
Judy Nolte Lensink
Patricia MacCorquodale

State University of New York Press

Published by
State University of New York Press, Albany

© 1988   State University of New York

For information, address State University of New York
Press, State University Plaza, Albany, N.Y., 12246

Library of Congress Cataloging in Publication Data

Changing our minds.

    Includes index.
    1. Feminism. 2. Women—Research. 3. Women's studies
—Methodology. 4. Knowledge, Theory of. I. Aiken,
Susan Hardy, 1943-
HQ1154.C454   1988   305.4'2   87-9975
ISBN 0-88706-618-6
ISBN 0-88706-619-4 (pbk.)

10 9 8 7 6 5 4 3 2

Contents

About the Editors

SUSAN HARDY AIKEN, Associate Professor of English, University of Arizona, has published widely in nineteenth- and twentieth-century literature and feminist criticism in such journals as *PMLA*, *Contemporary Literature*, and *Scandinavian Studies*. She is currently working on *Isak Dinesen and the Engendering of Narrative*, a book on the implications of gender and sexual difference in Dinesen's texts.

KAREN ANDERSON, Associate Professor of History, University of Arizona, specializes in the history of women, specifically women and work, and women and the family. The author of *Wartime Women: Sex Roles, Family Relations, and the Status of Women During World War II*, she is currently writing a book on minority group women in America entitled *Changing Woman: A History of Racial Ethnic Women in Modern America*.

MYRA DINNERSTEIN, Chairperson of Women's Studies and Director of the Southwest Institute for Research on Women at the University of Arizona, has directed a number of curriculum integration projects at both the elementary, secondary and university levels. She is co-author of "Initiating a Curriculum Integration Project: Lessons from the Campus and the Region," in *Women's Place in the Academy: Transforming the Liberal Arts* (1985) and has written other essays on women's studies and curriculum integration.

JUDY NOLTE LENSINK, Assistant Director of the curriculum project at the University of Arizona from which these essays came, is doing research on women's writing including "Expanding the Boundaries of Criticism: the Diary as Female Autobiography" in *Women's Studies: An Interdisciplinary Journal*, Summer 1987, as well as *The Diary of Emily Hawley Gillespie, 1858-1888: Typical Pattern, Atypical Perception* (in progress). She has also edited a collection of essays on Southwestern literature, *Old Southwest/New Southwest*.

PATRICIA MAC CORQUODALE, Associate Professor of Sociology, University of Arizona, is co-author of *Premarital Sexuality: Attitudes, Relationships, Behavior*. She specializes in the study of sex roles, ethnicity, human sexuality, and women in science and math. Her current research is focused on two areas: gender and justice, a study of inequities in legal outcomes and in the experiences of attorneys and judges; and gender and ethnic identities, a comparison of socialization and family relations in Mexican-American and Anglo families.

Contributors

LESLIE A. FLEMMING, Associate Professor of Oriental Studies, University of Arizona, is author of *Another Lonely Voice: The Urdu Short Stories of Saadat Hasan Manto* (1979). She was a Fulbright Fellow to India in 1982. She is currently doing research on interactions between Indian women and American missionaries in North India.

JERROLD E. HOGLE, Associate Professor of English, University of Arizona, was a member of the Steering Committee for the curriculum integration project. He also serves as one of the available consultants for the Southwest Institute for Research on Women. His scholarly work includes the forthcoming *Shelley's Process: Radical Transference and the Development of his Major Works*, and numerous essays and reviews on literary theory, Romantic Poetry, and English novels of the eighteenth and nineteenth centuries.

GARY F. JENSEN, Professor of Sociology, University of Arizona, is a noted scholar in the field of juvenile delinquency. In addition to numerous articles and book chapters, Jensen is co-author with Dean Rojek of *Delinquency: A Sociological View*, and an accompanying book of readings. He is currently finishing a research monograph on gender differences in the experiences of lawyers and clients.

DOUG MCADAM, Associate Professor of Sociology, University of Arizona, is the author of *Political Process and the Development of Black Insurgency, 1930-1970*. His research on social movements, gerontology, and privacy appears in numerous books and journals. A Guggenheim Fellowship in 1984 furthered his latest research project, a longitudinal study of activists. McAdam will highlight the gender differences in the consequences of civil rights participation in his forthcoming book, *Freedom Summer: The Idealists Revisited*.

PATRICK O'DONNELL, Associate Professor of English, University of Arizona, is the author of *John Hawkes* (1982), *Passionate Doubts: Designs of Interpretation in Contemporary American Fiction* (1986), and numerous articles and reviews on critical theory and twentieth-century American fiction.

LAWRENCE A. SCAFF, Associate Professor of Political Science, University of Arizona, specializes in political and social theory. His work, which focuses particularly on Max Weber, has appeared in the *American Political Science Review*, *The American Journal of Sociology*, *The British Journal of Sociology*, and elsewhere. His continuing research on Weber has been supported by grants from the German Academic Exchange Service, The Fulbright Foundation, and the National Endowment for the Humanities.

Acknowledgments

We would like to thank those who have made possible both the University of Arizona curriculum integration project and this book. We are particularly grateful to Gary Jensen, who first suggested that we do the book. The National Endowment for the Humanities provided funding for the faculty development project and John Stephenson, now President of Berea College, offered encouragement and wise advice as the project evaluator. The Women's Studies staff, Maureen Roen, Roxane Martell Jones, Jo Ann Troutman, and Mary Contreras, did their usual excellent job of providing essential support for the entire endeavor. Lynn Fleischman's discerning suggestions were invaluable. The many Women's Studies faculty who participated in the seminars contributed not only their scholarly expertise but their moral support, reaffirming for all of us the strength and importance of the women's studies community in our lives.

Introduction

Today more than ever, changing our minds—changing *the*
mind—is a woman's prerogative.

Shoshana Felman,
"Women and Madness: The
Critical Phallacy"

Telling Tales: Women and Traditional Constructions of Knowledge

On the issue of woman's relation to the traditional university
curriculum, as on so many other gender-inflected issues, Virginia
Woolf remains among our most perceptive commentators. Take, for
instance, one of the key parables of exclusion she recounts in the first
chapter of *A Room of One's Own*. Her narrator—a fictionalized
version of Woolf herself—is visiting "Oxbridge," composite of
those venerable British institutions of higher learning that for
centuries were bastions of exclusively male education. Strolling on
the campus one October morning, she has endured several humiliat-
ing adventures that underscore the handicap of female gender in such
a setting: as a woman she may not walk across the grass plots of the
college quadrangles reserved for male scholars, nor enter the famous
libraries, repositories of the "treasures" of Western culture, unless
she is "accompanied by a Fellow"—in both senses of the term.
Having experienced repeated rebukes for trespassing on these
prohibited precincts, she finds momentary solace in a luncheon,
during the course of which she happens to glance out the window.
There, surreptitiously crossing one of the very grass plots from
which she herself was summarily ejected, is a cat without a tail, a
creature whose unexpected appearance crystallizes for her all the
issues of gender and education on which she has been meditating: "as
I watched the Manx cat pause in the middle of the lawn as if it too
questioned the universe, something seemed lacking, something
seemed different. But what, ... I asked myself. And to answer that
question I had to think myself out of the room, back into the
past ... "—that past in which sexual difference, like race and class,
determined education, or the lack of it; that past in which women

were excluded from the institutions of higher learning and therefore
from the official constructions of "truth" and "knowledge" those
institutions systematically established and perpetuated. Considering
the cultural consequences of the traditional notion that for women,
as for Manx cats, anatomy is, as Freud put it, destiny, Woolf comes
to a wry conclusion: "It is strange what a difference a tail makes."[1]

Clearly, the "tale" of the missing "tail" points in several
directions at once. The multiple meanings of Woolf's playful pun
anticipate what contemporary feminist criticism has taught us about
woman's place in traditional androcentric canons and curricula and
about the possibilities of what Adrienne Rich, in a now-famous
phrase, has called the "re-vision" of those structures. First, one
recalls that historically, even before the existence of universities as
formal institutions, women in Western culture were largely prohibited from active participation—not to mention leadership—in
most public spheres, whether political, economic, legal, educational,
or even religious, given the pervasive influence of the Judaeo-
Christian tradition, with its male priestly castes and its predominantly androcentric Scriptures. That is, women were generally
excluded from the realms where public discourse among men shaped
what we have inherited and what our universities have institutionalized as *the* Western cultural tradition. Despite the many women who
have known the uses of subversive, unofficial power, and those
often-cited "exceptions" who even within patriarchal systems
obtained a measure of public, "legitimate" recognition—like Elizabeth I of England, monarch of an otherwise all-male government,
under whose reign, significantly, the general status and lot of most
women declined—the tales of our official histories, philosophical
and theological systems, literatures, sciences, and other academic
disciplines have narrated primarily aspects of the story of "man."
Accounts of those who transcended androcentric systems are,
moreover, tales only beginning to be told, or heard, with any
frequency, tales disconcertingly riddled by gaps and silences.
Traditional histories, and most male-authored texts canonized in the
secular scripture that is academia's received inheritance, have
generally represented women as marginal, secondary, subsidiary, or
derivative figures, defined almost entirely through their male
affiliations as the mothers, wives, daughters, sisters, or mistresses,
but rarely the leaders of men; rarely, even, independent agents in
their own right. Indeed, those who have claimed an autonomous

independence are often represented as unnatural or masculine figures, seductive or destructive or both, *disruptions* to be restrained or contained in the name of civilization, the family, religious piety, truth, law and order, and other such sacralized rubrics. In short, the exceptions in this tale of Western culture underscore the general rule of female anonymity.

Moreover, because virtually every major discipline developed in times when culturally-constructed gender roles were perceived as natural and inevitable, gender has seldom served as a key factor of scholarly analysis; until quite recently, with the advent of contemporary feminist inquiry, scholarship has been too often gender blind in the negative sense of that term, assuming the masculine as the human norm, presupposing that what was true of men must be true of women too. Unfortunately, Adrienne Rich's summary of the situation in 1973 still largely obtains: "There is no discipline that does not obscure and devalue the history and experience of women as a group."[2]

The intellectual distortions and falsifications inherent in this androcentric tale of Western culture and scholarship have seriously detrimental consequences for all students, but are especially devastating for women: lacking evidence of women's enormously varied and invaluable activities in history, their contributions to the shaping of culture, female students lack also the necessary models for their own growth beyond the traditional limits imposed on their sex. These lacks in turn impede their development of autonomy—of personal "tales" or life scripts that do not depend on identifying only with "great men" and hence on denying or repressing aspects of their own femaleness. Rich put the paradox thus: "As women have gradually and reluctantly been admitted into the mainstream of higher education, they have been made participants in a system that prepares men to take up roles of power in a man-centered society, that asks questions and teaches 'facts' generated by a male intellectual tradition, and that both subtly and openly confirms men as the leaders and shapers of human destiny both within and outside academe.... That all this is somehow 'natural' and reasonable is still an unconscious assumption even of many who grant that women's role in society is changing and that it needs to change."[3]

That much-needed change has been strikingly aided over the past two decades by the development of a vast new body of scholarship on women. Like the Manx cat, this scholarship at first appeared odd, even faintly comic, to those still firmly ensconced within the confines of traditional androcentric disciplines. Like the Manx cat, too, those who practiced this scholarship were often regarded (and in many cases are still regarded) with suspicion, as trespassers or transgressors, literally those who cross (illicitly) over fixed boundaries. Now, however, increasing numbers of academics are recognizing the positive possibilities of this kind of boundary crossing. Yet the boundaries themselves remain. Clearly, the superb efforts of individual feminist scholars cannot alone effect the transformation of the academy Rich so eloquently called for.

Woolf herself foresaw the problem: that institutional accep-tance of a few women—the invitation to join "the procession of the sons of educated men," but at the end of the line—did not assure any fundamental change within those institutions.[4] For the most recent generation of academic feminists who have attempted to bring critical possibilities offered by their unique vantage points to the academic tradition, her observations seem especially prescient. Although by the mid-1970s, over 5000 courses on women were offered and over 300 Women's Studies programs had been estab-lished on campuses throughout the United States,[5] feminist scholar-ship still occupied the margins of the androcentric academy, reaching only a small audience of students in courses outside the "mainstream" curriculum.[6]

To modify this curricular containment, Women's Studies scholars devised a dual strategy: to continue their groundbreaking research and criticism, challenging the androcentric paradigms that ratify the erasure of woman, and to incorporate basic feminist scholarship within traditional fields of knowledge by initiating scores of curriculum transformation projects in colleges and univer-sities throughout the country.[7] Though varied in design and duration, all these projects have sought not only to increase the amount of material on women presented in courses throughout the curriculum, but, more fundamentally, to encourage traditionally trained faculty to reformulate the conceptual frameworks of their disciplines, to acknowledge and analyze gender as a crucial organizing principle in human societies and cultural productions. It is axiomatic for such projects that the incorporation of scholarship on women into the academic mainstream will not only enrich traditional disciplines but initiate their transformation, that what is needed is a creative rethinking of their fundamental assumptions, epistemologies, and methodologies—a rewriting of the "tales" they have told themselves about themselves—as well as a reconsideration of those other boundaries, the disciplinary lines along which the traditional academy operates.

The Arizona Project

Among the earliest and most extensive of these projects was a four-year cross-disciplinary program at the University of Arizona, sponsored by the National Endowment for the Humanities. Regarded nationwide as a forerunner in the field of feminist curriculum transformation, this program was distinguished by its combination of a number of elements that have seldom coalesced in other such projects: its sheer size and duration, which enabled us to reach a broadly representative spectrum of the liberal arts professoriat; a target faculty group comprised almost entirely of men; an interdisciplinary format; and the frequency and intensity of the participants' interactions with each other and with the feminist scholars directing the project. Overall, 45 faculty members—42 men and 3 women— representing 13 departments participated in year-long activities designed to aid them in revising their courses. Central to the project were weekly seminars that provided a forum wherein faculty from a broad range of fields could meet with Women's Studies faculty to discuss major texts of feminist theory.[8] Concurrently, project participants engaged in additional guided reading and held consultations with feminist specialists in their individual disciplines about the relationship of the new scholarship on women to their pedagogy and research. By the end of the project the participants had prepared revised syllabi for approximately 80 courses. In addition, a number of them found their own research profoundly affected by their work in the project.

The essays collected herein represent some of the results of these transformations for the research, teaching, and lives of well-known scholars in a variety of disciplines in the social sciences and the humanities. There are, of course, a number of excellent books by feminist scholars that offer critiques of traditional systems of knowledge or analyze the techniques, processes, implications, or effects of curriculum integration. This collection is the first, however, to provide examples of significant scholarship by academics outside Women's Studies who, as a direct result of their participation in the curriculum integration process, have changed their minds, in the midst of their careers, about the foundations of their disciplines. These essays continue the multidisciplinary interaction begun in our seminars. They suggest, both in their individual voices and in the colloquy they implicitly create through their juxtapositions with each other, the telling transformations feminist analysis can effect in the contemporary academy, both within and across the traditional disciplines.

Border Crossings: The Essays

The interdisciplinary scope of the feminist project and of this book is not only essential to an adequate understanding of how pervasively human culture shapes and is shaped by sex/gender systems, or how thoroughly such systems shape and are shaped by our traditional ways of knowing. It is also an enactment of the premise that traditional academic disciplines, like other structures generated by patriarchal society, are interdependent parts of an androcentric system that obscures or negates the gestalts of women's experiences and perspectives. This system, as Hélène Cixous has argued, is grounded in a construction of "reality" as fundamentally divisible, a system of opposing, hierarchical categories founded on that most basic antinomy: male/female.[9] Yet despite the recognition that patriarchal ideologies, ontologies, and epistemologies—all those discourses of "truth" valorized and perpetuated by the academy—maintain themselves by reifying opposition as the principle of "order," most collections of feminist essays have remained discipline specific.[10] Without denying the necessity of such an intradisciplinary focus for the transformation of individual fields, we should also observe that field-specific collections necessarily elide the crucial question of how discipline-bound systems of knowledge may reinscribe the very categories they would interrogate. They elide as well the possibility of mutual illuminations across disciplinary boundaries. In putting together a series of essays from a variety of disciplinary perspectives, then, we hope not only to demonstrate the effects of changing minds within specific disciplines and to represent some of the range, variety, and intellectual vigor of intradisciplinary transformations of knowledge, but to stage precisely the sort of dialogue, or polylogue, that must occur among various systems of knowledge if the larger feminist project of cultural transformation is to succeed. This collection might be read, then, not only as a form of critical analysis—in the root sense both terms import of attention to *difference*(s)—but as an attempt at feminist re-membering, bringing together what the patriarchal academy would take, and keep, apart.

The following essays, whatever their unique theoretical perspectives and methodologies, all share a commitment to asking crucial questions about the cultural construction of gender and the gendered construction of culture. All draw on more than one field of knowledge. And all illuminate and modify each other in multiply significant ways. In what follows, we would like to indicate a few of the more salient of those mutual illuminations, to uncover points of permeability in the disciplinary boundaries by which the academy structures knowledge.

In analyzing the implications of traditional definitions of "the political" in "From Silence to Voice: Reflections on Feminism in Political Theory," Lawrence Scaff opens an inquiry that, either explicitly or implicitly, occupies all the essayists in the volume. Scaff draws on philosophy, literature, and political science to argue that political theory has historically acted as a discourse of domination: "a protective device . . . and a form of enticement." Seeking to elude the mystifications that such a discourse produces, feminism has offered four major responses to traditional political theory: rejectionist, critical, appropriative, and synthetic. Scaff considers the implications of each strategy, suggesting the particular value of a synthetic approach that combines an empirical criticism founded in female experience *and* a reformulation of the very concepts of the "political" and the "theoretical."

Scaff's recognition of the links between the discourse of politics and the politics of discourse intersects at a number of levels with Patrick O'Donnell's "Becoming Discourse: Eudora Welty's 'Petrified Man'." Combining psychoanalytic and linguistic theory with literary criticism, and drawing on the speculations of French theorists like Hélène Cixous and Luce Irigaray, O'Donnell analyzes how language and systems of representation interact with other cultural systems. Both Scaff and O'Donnell are concerned with the extent to which "the language we use to speak, to write with, to articulate our readings," whether of literature or politics, is "constricted by a repressive cultural order that authorizes patriarchy" and with the ways that "given political or social realities affect language itself" (O'Donnell, pp. 1-2). Just as Scaff reinterprets traditional political theory, O'Donnell's speculations lead to a provocative and original reinterpretation of Welty's 'Petrified Man' that also invites a comprehensive rereading of Welty as a woman writer and, in a larger sense, of the ways women's unique relations to the dominant androcentric culture may generate a different way with language and a discourse of subversion.

O'Donnell's focus on the question of difference between men's and women's "readings" of culture shares, in its turn, some of the chief concerns of Leslie Flemming's "New Visions, New Methods: The Mainstreaming Experience in Retrospect," an autobiographical reflection on the ways feminist research has transformed not only her work in Oriental Studies, but also her life. It is a narrative whose trajectory will seem intensely familiar to other academic women who came into a knowledge of feminist scholarship after years of unexamined, if uneasy, participation in the disciplines of the patriarchal academy. From a theoretical perspective, Flemming's essay raises with striking immediacy the question of whether men and women, by virtue of their different, gender-coded relations to the dominant cultural traditions and institutions, differ in their responses to feminist scholarship. One possible difference, even within the borders of this book, will be immediately evident: Flemming's essay, the only one in the collection except our own that is authored by a woman, is also the most explicitly personal. This may, of course, be fortuitous. We would certainly hesitate to draw any essentialist conclusions from it, especially since most academic women have been trained to "write like men" and to value such discourse, since all our male contributors are also highly sensitive to the implications of their own discursive choices, and since many men experienced and talked about personal transformations. Yet the difference does point out how difficult it is, even on the part of the most sympathetic academics, to elude the power of that academic myth Catharine MacKinnon has called "aperspectivity": the traditionally-sanctioned intellectual assumption that distance assures more accurate access to and representation of "truth," that the scholar should or could remain neutral, impersonal, objective, and *divorced from the subject* in both senses of the phrase. By placing Flemming's essay at the center of the collection, we hope to suggest that "the personal" remains at the core of every form of discourse. We would insist, finally, on the inseparability of the emotional and the cognitive, the confessional and the professional, even in those analyses that seem most abstracted from subjectivity. The separation of "personal" from "academic," subject from object, is another of those artificial oppositions that feminist theory would interrogate. In fact, the subjective nature of epistemological transformation is everywhere apparent in all the essays here. As Flemming's chapter eloquently confirms, to transform one's way of knowing is inevitably to transform oneself. In some sense all criticism is, after all, a form of autobiography, and autobiography a kind of criticism.

These questions about the intersections of the personal and the professional, the subjective and the objective, are crucial as well for Doug McAdam's "Gender Implications of the Traditional Academic Conception of the Political." As his title suggests, McAdam shares with Scaff and O'Donnell a concern with the ways *a priori* discursive categories shape our ways of knowing "reality." Like Scaff, McAdam seeks to redefine "the political," arguing that traditional definitions that would make that term identical with "public" both perpetuate a problematic opposition between "public" and "private" and foster a false division within the social sciences. Maintenance of this division not only narrows the content of political sociology to the examination of institutionalized politics and deemphasizes noninstitutional social movements, but also obscures the connections between "public" and "private" politics. In questioning the gender implications of such traditional theories, McAdam explores how including female power and action in one's analyses forces a reconceptualization of the whole meaning of politics and a restructuring of the field of political sociology.

Like Flemming, McAdam recognizes the truth of feminism's well-known insistence that "the personal is the political." In so doing he makes compelling claims for the permeability and mutuality of those areas of human experience traditionally labelled "public" and "private." Similar recognitions are inherent in the essays by Gary Jensen and Jerrold Hogle. Jensen's "Mainstreaming and the Sociology of Deviance" asks, among other things, how personality traits of individual adolescents are shaped by cultural codes that underwrite public adult behaviors and institutions. While recognizing the importance of feminist contributions to the sociology of deviance for bringing attention to gender as a factor of analysis, Jensen takes issue with those theorists who portray women as becoming increasingly similar to men in deviant behaviors. Jensen's review of empirical evidence supports his argument that girls commit fewer, and different kinds of, crimes than their male counterparts—a difference he attributes to the socialization processes that emphasize caring and nurturance for girls and encourage aggressive, competitive behavior in boys. Jensen demonstrates the extent to which "the adolescent male world" of contemporary American society (like the Western world more generally) encourages boys to value "pervasive competition, challenge, interpersonal aggression, and violence"—in other words, the very types of behavior most closely associated with criminal deviance. Like other contributors to this volume, Jensen focuses attention on the power of discursive categories in shaping cultural meanings. So pervasive, for example, is the association of maleness with violence that even the most eminent traditional sociologists of deviance, including some feminists, have tended to defend such socially disruptive behavior as acceptable because it represents the "masculine norm." "It just happens," as Jensen wryly remarks, "that those norms call for or justify behavior which conflicts with the law." Such sociologists must thus engage in a curious kind of linguistic double-think: "in dealing with a predominantly 'male' form of behavior" they tend "to transform it in ways which make it appear to be 'good.' " Thus "deviance is transformed into conformity . . . injustice into justice" (Jensen, p. 15).

Jensen's research intersects in remarkable ways with Hogle's analysis of the complex relations of the traditional Western literary canon to certain recurrent cultural constructs of "what it is properly 'masculine' or 'effeminate' to do, possess, be, or desire" (Hogle, p. 3). Drawing on historiography and cultural anthropology as well as psychoanalysis and literary theory, Hogle suggests that "unless we study how gender-based designations and repressions limit writers, characters, and modes of description, we cannot grasp larger issues: how a culturally determined 'style makes the man' or woman in a text and a social arena; and how that distinction is used to drain power from the members of one gender into those of another" in both text and society (Hogle, p. 4). Using *Hamlet* as a paradigm, Hogle observes that many of our most honored masterworks celebrate the subject of male violence, territoriality, and competition, surrounding it with a discourse on honor that operates precisely by devaluing or erasing the feminine. Thus, given "the cultural discourse in which [Hamlet] must fashion a 'self,'" hesitation to kill can be contemptuously labelled as "the kind of gainsgiving as would perhaps trouble a woman"—a phrase that resonates richly with Jensen's observation that the contemporary adolescent male who seeks to avoid violent encounters "risks being called . . . a 'pussy'" (p. 101). Jensen's suggestion that violent competitiveness is quintessentially "adolescent male" behavior, and directly related to criminal deviance, casts ironic new light on literary traditions that discount woman and "women's subjects" as trivial while exalting warfare and other forms of violence as important and serious concerns, the very essence of "the heroic" in genre, character, and theme. Taken together, Jensen's and Hogle's analyses raise important questions about the psychosocial foundations of precisely such revered androcentric terms as "honor" and "heroism."

We have concluded this collection with our own co-authored essay, tracing the changes of *our* thinking throughout the course of the project. In bringing together five voices from four different fields, "Trying Transformations: The Problematics of Curriculum Integration" reenacts the interdisciplinary premises of the entire book and seeks a discourse simultaneously theoretical and personal. Considering the complexities and ambiguities inherent in efforts to transform the academy, the essay analyzes a variety of related issues, all of which intersect, in diverse ways, with the inquiries of our contributors: the debate between essentialist and nonessentialist views of gender differences, the question of subjectivity versus objectivity, the differential levels of receptiveness to feminist scholarship, the expenditure of feminist energies in transforming received structures of knowledge, and the degree to which such transformations are possible within the traditional academy.

In putting together a collection that seeks to address the omissions, gaps, and silences imposed by androcentric institutions and epistemologies, we are acutely aware of the gaps and silences that remain within our own text: the relative dearth of attention, for example, to questions of racial, class, or ethnic differences, or to lesbian sexuality. While these lacks reflect the conditions under which the book took shape (see note 8), they nevertheless constitute a limitation that requires recognition, especially because one of the most pressing concerns of contemporary feminisms must be to address precisely the implications of the differences among women, the diversities of social and cultural contexts within which gender is constituted and constituent, and the danger of the sorts of totalizing pronouncements about these issues that risk reifying the very hegemonic structures they would contest. In this, as in other ways, we would acknowledge the tentative and admittedly partial nature of this collection: we claim no more than to add several lines of inquiry to the many—each necessarily incomplete—that make up the complex weave of contemporary feminist thought. Nevertheless, we hope that the essays herein demonstrate the value of the interdisciplinary premise with which feminist research and criticism begin: that what seem disparate threads can, when seen from a different perspective, turn out to be part of a larger tapestry, a text(ile) in which the weave of differences makes up a new whole that can suggest something of what a transformed academy might be like.

Notes

1. Virginia Woolf, *A Room of One's Own* (New York: Harcourt, Brace, and World, 1929), pp. 11-13.

2. Adrienne Rich, "Toward a Woman-Centered University," in *On Lies, Secrets, and Silence: Selected Prose, 1966-1978* (New York: Norton, 1979), p. 134.

3. Rich, "Toward a Woman-Centered University," in *Lies*, p. 127.

4. Virginia Woolf, *Three Guineas* (London: The Hogarth Press, 1938), p. 206.

5. See Florence Howe, "Women and the Power of Education," *American Association for Higher Education Bulletin* 33 (1981).

6. In 1979, with support from the National Endowment for the Humanities, we distributed evaluation forms to students in history, English, and philosophy courses to assess how much material on women they included. The results of this survey showed that a vast majority of students received almost no information about women except in courses taught by Women's Studies faculty. Reports from feminist scholars at other institutions confirm that our findings are typical of universities throughout the country.

7. For a thorough analysis of both sorts of project, see Ellen Carol DuBois, Gail Paradise Kelly, Elizabeth Lapovsky Kennedy, Carolyn W. Korssmeyer, and Lillian S. Robinson, *Feminist Scholarship: A Kindling in the Groves of Academe* (Urbana and Chicago: University of Illinois Press, 1985).

8. The University of Arizona is a large (30,000 students, 1200 faculty) research institution without a history of faculty development focused on teaching improvement. Our project was virtually the first on this campus to stress such development. It began in 1981. Each year, a Steering Committee of Women's Studies faculty conducted interdisciplinary seminars in feminist theory and pedagogy for approximately ten participants. During the last two years the Steering Committee added three men, former participants in the program, to help plan and reorganize the readings of subsequent seminars, but except for occasional presentations, they were not involved in the seminars themselves. Core readings included—to name only a few examples—texts by Nancy Chodorow, Bonnie Thornton Dill, Adrienne Rich, and Heidi Hartmann; Michelle Zimbalist Rosaldo's theoretical overview to *Women, Culture, and Society* and other readings from that collection; literary criticism by Annette Kolodny and Elaine Showalter; and selections from *The New French Feminisms* and *The Future of Difference*. Further examples are mentioned in our concluding essay, passim. In addition to their work in the seminars, participants prepared annotated bibliographies of readings in feminist scholarship in their fields, consulted systematically with Women's Studies faculty in their disciplines, and attended lectures and workshops led by a series of well-known visiting feminist scholars.

Because the conditions of the NEH grant stipulated the local institutionalization of results, and because we sought a permanent impact, we decided to focus only on tenured faculty during the first three years of the project, reasoning that they would be more likely to remain at the university than would untenured faculty members. During the fourth, extension year, however, we were able to include untenured faculty. Because over 90 percent of tenured faculty in the fields we dealt with were men, most of our project participants (42 of 45) were male. Also reflective of the academy in general was the fact that most of these men were white and middle class. While it can be argued that our choice of such participants may have guaranteed high levels of faculty resistance to change, this group nevertheless epitomizes what feminists face in one widespread type of university. These men are the major power brokers of the academy. To try to change their minds is arguably to take on the toughest challenge faced by feminist educators. For an account of the problematics of such efforts, see our concluding essay.

At the end of the semester in which participants taught the course targeted for integration, we administered evaluations to measure the degree of change in their classes as a result of their work in the program. Evaluations were also collected for a control group of unchanged courses matched according to size, level, and department. The student evaluations indicate that the project was successful on two accounts: (1) courses targeted for change included more material on women in assigned readings, syllabus topics, lectures, and class discussions; and (2) generally, students reacted positively to these materials, becoming more aware of women's issues and wanting similar courses to contain more such material.

9. Cixous, "Sorties," in Hélène Cixous and Catherine Clement, *La Jeune Née*; trans. as *The Newly Born Woman*, trans. Betsy Wing (Minneapolis: University of Minnesota Press, 1986), pp. 63-64.

10. There are exceptions to this generalization. For examples, see *The Prism of Sex*, ed. Julia A. Sherman and Evelyn Torton Beck (Madison: University of Wisconsin, 1977); *Men's Studies Modified: The Impact of Feminism on the Academic Disciplines*, ed. Dale Spender (Oxford: Pergamon Press, 1981); *A Feminist Perspective in the Academy: The Difference It Makes*, ed. Elizabeth Langland and Walter Gove (Chicago: University of Chicago Press, 1983). All these texts are primarily authored by feminist women. *Men in Feminism*, ed. Alice Jardine and Paul Smith (New York and London: Methuen, 1987), which appeared after this book went to press, developed largely out of sessions on the topic at a conference of the Modern Language Association.

LAWRENCE A. SCAFF

1. From Silence to Voice: Reflections on Feminism in Political Theory

A deep and powerful alto voice of the kind one sometimes hears
in the theater can suddenly raise the curtain upon possibilities in
which we usually do not believe.

Nietzsche

In its dialogue with feminism the form of inquiry generally
known in the Western philosophical tradition as "political theory"
starts with two counts against it. With rare exceptions its subject
matter—"politics"—and the preferred abstract categories and theoretical language it has traditionally used to order that subject matter
have systematically excluded women. For feminism exclusion is
especially marked in political theory conceived as a reconstructed
"tradition" of discourse, a conversation for the initiated across time
and space, an idea, despite recent pummelings, that still maintains a
tenacious grip on the theoretical vocation. But male-centered
discourse is also characteristic of much of contemporary "analytic"
political theory, where, for instance, models of "rational man" seem
to display precisely those familiar qualities of egoistic "rationality"
that have dominated the phallocentric tradition and none of the
alternatives that feminists have advanced as part of a revisionist
androgynous conception of rational *human* choice. Even the exceptions among political theorists—say, Plato and Mill, to stay with
figures from the traditional canon—only serve to demonstrate the
rule: students of the subject have heard endless favorable commentary by Plato's epigones on his promise in the *Republic* to create a
world safe for philosophy, but scarcely a whisper about his more
daring projection of a world safe for women, much less comment on

1

the probable relationship between the two. Or we have been treated to countless discussions of Mill's principle of liberty in *On Liberty*, but only to uneasy silence on the more controversial defense of perfect equality of gender in *The Subjection of Women*, a defense that surely challenges the notion of liberty as a privileged good (and one whose implications Mill himself may not have fully understood).[1]

More is at stake than some kind of habitual reflex or historically conditioned exclusion, however. Theoretical discourse itself—the most abstract, general and fundamental aspect of knowledge—has often appeared to feminism as a male domain whose function has been to arrogate power by defining, enforcing, and preserving exclusionary vocabularies. "Theory" itself thus becomes suspect as a "discourse of domination," and those spheres of human achievement which are most essentially theoretical—metaphysics, mathematics, musical composition—are assigned special standing as the obsessive province of "higher" male powers.[2] What is reserved for women in this view, of course, is all that is "lower," that is to say more practical, everyday, earthly, organic, natural, subjective, responsive, caring, obedient—and human. Our deepest myths betray this alignment of characteristics, and not only in the texts of political theory: for instance, when Thomas Mann's most cerebral composer, Adrian Leverkuhn, collapses at the end of *Doctor Faustus*, repeating Nietzsche's fall, his creative powers shattered by fanatical intellection, he is enveloped by a protective body of women whose visible caring is symbolically speechless. This imagined terminus of the Western musical aesthetic which is at the same time a death knell for the theoretical mind, is not invoked to mark the sounding of a different, alto voice. It issues instead only in silence. The return of Leverkuhn-Faust to the maternal protection "from whence he came" is simply the fading away of theoretical discourse in favor of natural necessity. And Mann's ending suggests that it is the memory of that discourse, of what it was and had become, that continues to dominate all future theoretical imagination.

Perhaps I exaggerate. But a reflection on feminism's relationship to political theory that begins with Nietzsche, that petulant and tasteless subverter of "the eternal feminine," the "old earth-shaker sing[ing] his aria in the lowest depths, deep as a bellowing bull,"[3] must begin *in extremis*, with a postulated negation of political theory. It must start with the strongest and worst possible case against political theory, from the feminist point of view. That case takes shape, I want to suggest, around a double vision of what political theory has become in the course of its development. For a critical feminism it has become both a protective device insuring male political and theoretical dominance and a form of enticement promising "participation" while in fact guaranteeing female acquiescence. One is intimately connected to the other: in establishing the terms or rules of authoritative discourse, the project of Western political theory also holds out the elusive prospect of acquiring power.

We see the meaning of this double vision and its interconnections amplified to a high pitch of intensity in some of the most legendary accomplishments in political theory. Consider, for example, the relentless probing of the dynamics of mastery over the world of necessity and fortune in Machiavelli's passages on *virtu*. For Machiavelli it is always a matter of opposing the active, innovative, scheming, verbal improvisations of *virtu* to resistant, mute, and fickle realities. The triumph of masculine initiative, aided by wily theory, is a triumph of will over woman. In Machiavelli's familiar lines:

> I certainly think it is better to be impetuous than cautious, for fortune is a woman, and it is necessary, if you wish to master her, to conquer her by force; and it can be seen that she lets herself be overcome by the bold rather than by those who proceed coldly. And therefore, like a woman, she is always a friend to the young, because they are less cautious, fiercer, and master her with greater audacity.[4]

Machiavelli's human-all-too-human metaphor of action is remarkable for breaking down distinctions which might be taken for granted as part of any "moral order": force and consent, violence and persuasion, deceit and authenticity, means and ends, rape and love. The seduction of the goddess *fortuna* is initiated by the man of action armed with an instrumental theory—Machiavelli's—which blurs responsibility and culpability. Is her resistance complete and uncomprising? Or does she "let herself be overcome?"

What is alarming about Machiavelli's example is not only the intentional confusion, but also the didactic lesson: sexual conquest becomes a kind of preparation for political mastery. The function of this preparation, confined at first to the private realm, is to protect the male domain of objective, public life, placing the female symbols of subjectivity within the circle of sexual and domestic domination. Confinement is repeated and reinforced by the theory—the text— itself, a theory that succeeds on its shimmering surfaces in including women, but as object, as possession. When earthly women rather than goddesses appear in *The Prince*, Machiavelli only warns his spellbinding political artist-seducer to abstain "from interfering with the property of his citizens and subjects or with their women."[5] The seduction is now complete. After it comes a projection of external power based upon an internal *symphonia domestica* which is, to be sure, the classic formula for republican realism: domestic harmony coupled to imperial power.

But is it a jest? What kind of astonishment and laughter might be provoked by Machiavelli's subjection of women? The clearest answer comes not from *The Prince*, but from Machiavelli's finest comedy, *Mandragola*, in which the theorist-counsellor impersona- tor, Ligurio, demonstrates how the discourse of domination can be made to conquer all. Since the comedy is motivated by impending seduction, not to say prurience, it forms the perfect illustration of *virtu* in practice, following the line of thought in *The Prince*. Voluble Ligurio, never at a loss for words, schemes successfully to bed the fair, married, and reticent Lucrezia with his friend Callimaco. The *comedia* is pure politics, with woman as the prize. Always at a loss for words that are her own, Lucrezia resigns herself to a necessity ("God's will," she says) which is in fact conjured from the most human of materials: greed, passion, stupidity, confusion, hushed innocence. Conjuring the entrapment is the specific achievement of the masculine theoretical imagination. But success presupposes an absence, a voiceless and willess "other." Far from making "great advances toward self-conscious immorality" through the play,[6] Lucrezia's is a personality we can never get to know, for it lacks autonomous form, development, or intention. It exists merely as a phantasm of male desire.

Machiavelli's allegorical political drama ends in apparent unity, marred only by woman's acquiescence to entrapment. We are invited to overlook this dangerous "only" in the interest of comic satisfaction and admiration for the feats of theory. But when playfulness is replaced by seriousness, dangers cannot be so easily swept aside. For example, Ligurio's darker counterpart, Mephisto- pheles, establishes a different tone and sets a more deadly struggle in motion, as can be seen immediately in the first gender-specific encounter of Goethe's *Faust*.[7]

> Faust: Beautiful lady, I wonder if I may offer my arm to escort you anywhere?
> Margaret: I'm neither a lady, nor am I pretty, and I know my own way home.

The encounter takes on archetypal significance. It is the violation of woman's assertion of self-knowledge that turns this alternative seduction into tragedy. The possibility of finding a different, woman's voice, briefly glimpsed in the first encounter, is quickly cut short by the cunning of a discourse of domination in the service of desire. The thought that Machiavelli's wit might also be emplotted with a tragic outcome makes his "invitation" to woman all the more suspect. The invitation is not merely a harmless joke.

Because of his antifeminist instincts, Nietzsche saw through to the meaning of these representations in the "culture of realism," as he called it. They were a way of staking out the boundaries of male "courage," a courage to confront "reason in reality," rather than yielding to the "feminine" narcotic of an "escape into the ideal." For Nietzsche, Plato followed the latter path, creating philosophy as a "higher swindle"—the political philosophy that had dared to imagine a kind of equal membership for women. Contrasted to Machiavelli and before him Thucydides, this was the beginning of cultural "decadence" in Nietzsche's language. That language recapitulated the mythical association of the appearance of woman as a public participant with the appearance of both "morality" (i.e., a morality of *ressentiment*) and the ideology of social "progress."[8]

Defenders of political theory's integrity might reply to these unconventional charges in any number of ways: by straightforward denial, by praise for other nonrealistic conceptions of their favorite subject matter, by attacks on the apparent immorality and nihilism of Machiavelli's and Nietzsche's views, or by a dialectical criticism. With respect to the last kind of response, feminist contemporaries of Nietzsche clearly saw the two-faced potentialities and dangers early on: Looking upon the sinister side of his thinking, Hedwig Dohm commented that "Nietzsche-Machiavelli gives woman advice about how to carry on," but then concluded, "Is a more powerful argument for the modern woman's movement thinkable than

Nietzsche's opinion [about women]?"⁹ This sort of dialectical rejoinder is more interesting than the alternatives, for it raises the central questions for political theory: what has been *feminist* theory's response to the worst-case state of affairs I have described? What conclusions have been drawn about and for political theory, including feminism's own political theory?

Anyone who has attempted to teach a course in political theory that includes feminist materials will have quickly discovered that there is no single, authoritative feminist political *Weltanschauung* or theory, and that the answer to these questions therefore has not been unified. Instead, an array of possible answers has emerged, coalescing for the most part around four types of positions: the wholesale rejection of political theory as it has been practiced until now; criticism of the tradition it represents; appropriation of selected elements from political theory; or attempts at theoretical synthesis based sometime upon older models. These positions with respect to political theory need not be mutually exclusive, nor can they be arrayed along a neat ideological continuum. Yet within contemporary feminism there is considerable debate among them, for each can be said to reflect the deepest hopes, purposes, and commitments of a particular community of feminist experience.

At its core the first of these positions has viewed political theory with considerable skepticism, as if to say even the first encounter with it will speak the fateful language of male expectations. To enter the dialogue is already to concede far too much. Thus, before crossing the threshold of communication care must be taken to invent a new language, a "language of the body," grounded in female being and time and purged of corrupting traditional male forms.¹⁰ In its most radical manifestations, this view finds little more than the threat of humiliation and subordination in the canonical texts of Western political thought. The "tradition" so-called is not merely useless; it is irretrievably compromised.

Ironically, rejection in its own way tends to follow one path already set forth in the tradition: the utopian path. Using the imagery employed above, one of its responses to the Nietzschean taunts might be characterized as something like Platonic institution-building. The preferred "new order for the age" comes to be roughly Plato's republic with men confined to an androceum. Evidently in this view writers like Nietzsche and Machiavelli were largely correct—at least about what used to be seriously discussed as "the nature of man." The inverted symmetry of the new political order can only be considered appropriately classical. It requires a mere switch in the gender of imperial power. But the question that this feminism wants to raise is, can power (and with it politics) be transformed along heretofore unknown dimensions of human experience? Is it possible that it might be so transformed in a future feminist culture?[11]

The questions posed by the remaining three positions are perhaps less speculative. While all urge a dialogue with the intellectual resources of political theory, they register certain differences about the form engagement should take. The "critical" approach to political theory is best understood as an attempt to unmask the tradition by revealing its misogynist errors, distortions and omissions.[12] This requires criticism in the narrow sense: a demonstration of the shocking *theoretical* justification of woman's subjugation in an Aristotle, an Aquinas, a Nietzsche. Recourse to an investigation of political theory, usually as a historical subject, is deemed pertinent if for no other reason than to show the continuities and innovations of the Western mind and especially the modern triumph of women despite remarkably petty arguments and shabby treatment in the tradition from which they emerged.

It is a short step from criticism of the tradition to appropriation of its concepts and arguments for feminist purposes, and in fact a good deal of feminist writing combines the two.[13] The distinctive intention of this position is to borrow and reconstruct political (and ethical) arguments—e.g., Aristotle's concept of citizenship or Rousseau's advocacy of participation—notwithstanding the use to which they have been put historically in efforts to subjugate women. The source of difficulty is not the argument per se, it is claimed, but rather some other set of mistaken epistemological beliefs, false assumptions about "woman's nature," or unproven assertions of biological or genetic determinism.[14] Appropriating ideas that are serviceable for feminism presupposes, then, not merely that the useful can be separated from the superfluous, but that the truths perceived by feminism can be logically detached with advantage from their traditional epistemological foundations. The assumption that the latter must be fundamental or primary, grounding all principled arguments, has obscured the validity of women's historical experience of injustice. The language of political theory can be borrowed, interpreted, restated in order to make that experience

intelligible. There is, in this view, no other reasonable alternative—
or, what is the same thing, all other alternatives remain at the level of
pure experience and are therefore beyond the bounds of rational,
conceptual discourse.

One difficulty with the borrowing of arguments and concepts is
that it can become *only* a kind of strategy, a way of proceeding, rather
than a coherent assemblage of well-founded, integrated arguments
and principles. In short, it is not yet a theory. The attempt at
synthesis addresses this difficulty: its ultimate aim is formation of a
feminist theory, appropriately grounded in experience, yet capable
of transforming that experience with the power and conceptual rigor
displayed by other modes of theorizing.[15] This particular response to
political theory is innovative: it does not seek to define itself in terms
of any of the existing political ideologies—liberalism, socialism,
marxism, and the like—but instead proposes to articulate a new,
distinctive, synthetic mode of feminist theory outside the boundaries of the traditional canon, yet at the same level of mastery as its
theoretical predecessors. In this sense the history of political theory
becomes a repository for models and analogies demonstrating what a
feminist theory might be like. Emerging feminist political theory is
conceived to be similar to predecessors in form, while differing in
content. It sees itself to be the only genuine successor to all forms of
radical critique. Or, in the terms I have chosen to emphasize, it seeks
to become the authentic "alto voice" now conscious of knowing its
"own way home."

Regardless of the precise nature of feminism's current response
to the history and language of political theory, it seems that the
most promising prescription for avoiding a reenactment of past
failures lies in maintaining a critical dialogue with political theory.
Proponents of dialogue, in whatever form, appear to agree on a
common starting point. What Pateman says about the relations
between feminism and democratic theory can be said with equal
force about the relations between feminism and political theory in
general; namely, that a critical feminism provides the "most
important challange and most comprehensive critique" of the
tradition of political thought.[16] The challenge and critique proceed at
two levels. At what might be called the empirical level, criticism
develops through an appeal to the particularity of women's experience, while at the theoretical level, critical content is defined by an
attempt to revise conceptions of the "political" and the "theoreti-

cal" itself in light of an understanding of this experience. A distinctive feminist theory will emerge only when these two levels have been unified—something that has not yet occurred. But given the present level of development in feminist theory, its current project can be described as above all critical and radical: its overriding intention is to criticize presuppositions, and this variety of criticism is itself an important form of theorizing.[17]

The meaning and promise of a feminist dialogue with political theory can be illuminated by considering how and why a critical feminism renders familiar and apparently uncontroversial issues problematic in a new way. Take, for instance, the closely related problems of justice, the nature of the family, and the relationship between public and private in a major theoretical text, such as Hegel's *Philosophy of Right*. What would a critical feminist reading reveal about Hegel's famous argument?

In his political philosophy of "right" or "law" Hegel conceives the state developing out of two opposed "moments" in the general economy of ethical life: the family, whose members are bound together by a kind of particular altruism, and civil society, in which activities are characterized conversely by a generalized egoism. Hegel makes clear that his aim is the redefinition of Plato's achievement in the *Republic*; that is, creation of the "pure universality" or "substantiality" of a collective and public life, based upon justice, but now subsuming elements of what he calls "self-subsistent particularity" (e.g., the family) as the necessary first moment of human association. From Hegel's point of view Plato's mistake—a mistake leading to idealization of the Greek ethical life—was to attempt to control such "negative" elements through exclusion, as becomes visible in Plato's insistence upon a community of wives for his guardians, prohibition of private property, and so forth.[18]

Hegel's full reply to Plato requires, in brief, developing a conception of unity out of difference, negation, and opposition. As Greek philosophy instructed Western thought, the most fundamental elements of opposition are found in *gender*, and therefore in the microcosmic embodiment of gendered relations—the family. Accepting this assumption, Hegel expresses the idea in one central passage, whose characteristic obscurity should not blind us to its importance and meaning:

Thus one sex is mind in its self-diremption into explicit personal self-subsistence and the knowledge and volition of free universality, *i.e.* the self-consciousness of conceptual thought and the volition of the objective final end. The other sex is mind maintaining itself in unity as knowledge and volition of the substantive, but knowledge and volition in the form of concrete individuality and feeling. In relation to externality, the former is powerful and active, the latter passive and subjective.

The polarization of male and female "being" could hardly be more explicit. But Hegel does not stop here, for this final aim is to ground characterological-political claims on this ontology:

> It follows that man has his actual substantive life in the state, in learning, and so forth, as well as in labour and struggle with the external world and with himself so that it is only out of his diremption that he fights his way to self-subsistent unity with himself. In the family he has a tranquil intuition and this unity, and there he lives a subjective ethical life on the plane of feeling. Woman, on the other hand, has her substantive destiny in the family, and to be imbued with family piety is her ethical frame of mind.[19]

Clearly Hegel wants to say that woman's voice is walled in by certain ethical imperatives: subjectivity, passivity, concreteness, feeling, tranquility, intuition—the language is familiar enough. The "destiny" of woman, the expression of "family piety," is the negation of "free universality": it can be neither free nor universal, only a unity, but at the "lower" level of feeling. The "true" unity of mind and morality, hence the very possibility of achieving fully-developed personality or the objectification of the self, is reserved for those Faustian struggles of man with self and world.

What is remarkable in Hegel's thinking is not so much the opposition between "man" and "other," which we have encountered before, but rather Hegel's assumption that transformation to "higher" forms of the just political life (and personality), the ceaseless dynamic of creation and cancellation, presupposes this *particular* form for woman and the family. Stated somewhat brusquely, without the subjectivity of woman enshrined in the family as the first moment of "ethical life," the ensuing moments— negative and positive—leading to free, objective universality and the political life of the state become merely imaginary. Possibilities for self-development and political transformation evaporate. Beginning and ending are thus necessarily unified. Hegel must imagine woman as he does in order to generate the masculine state. If woman refuses to conform to his imagination, his entire political project melts into easy-going incoherence. In this respect Hegel's ontology is entirely representative of the tradition: to conceive of woman in contrary terms is to call into question the founding principles of Western politics.

Now I am not interested in rescuing Hegel's argument, if it could be rescued at all, but I do wish to suggest, as a result of this sort of "thought experiment" that it might be possible for a critical feminism to retain the developmental perspective of the argument while altering its contents. If the central distinctions of Hegel's first "moment" in the family are attached not to gender but to properties of mind or self, for example, then form might still unfold with altered contents, without risking the seductive allure of Hegel's invitation to the gendered experience of "unity" and its preconditions. It is not inappropriate to suggest this as one new direction chosen by feminist criticism, a direction that obviously alters not merely woman's position, but the nature of the formation of character and the family, and, *as a consequence*, the nature of public and political life.

As feminist political theory gains in self-confidence, it will inevitably explore possibilities beyond those glimpsed by a new reading of a figure like Hegel. But as it does so, unresolved dilemmas will return to enliven the dialogue between feminism and the tradition of political theory. In passing from feminism's present accomplishments to reflections upon its probable future, there appear to be two dilemmas that will attract attention.

It is not entirely clear in the first place whether the different voice of feminism will choose to treat "woman" as a determinate ontological category or as a sociohistorical configuration of characteristics and possibilities. The second alternative may be preferred (I prefer it myself) because of its support for radical conceptions of selfhood and freedom, not to mention its break with some of the most pernicious patriarchal stereotyping. But assertions of woman's distinctiveness and "special nature," her irreplaceable "being," seem destined in one form or another to comfort even the fair-weather champions of feminism, to say nothing of the tough-minded advocates. The unfortunate difficulty, as the ambivalent feminist reception of Gilligan's recent work demonstrates, is to find a clear and principled basis for woman's "difference" that both preserves the argument for justice and equal rights but avoids abetting the standard case for women's subjection made by a figure like Hegel.[20] It is not self-evident that this balance can be struck, or even that the attempt is well-advised, particularly in the absence of any coherent distinction between the "natural" and the "social."

The second dilemma that is perhaps more obscure than the first, though no less serious, appears at feminism's center in the category of the "political" itself: what is the nature of the new feminist politics? Is it merely a replication of our standard market-based models of politics, in which all relevant action is reduced essentially to bargaining for competitive advantage in a situation of scarce resources and limited political goods? Or does it portend a leap beyond the ordinary into a novel realm of political consciousness? To adopt the slogan "the personal _is_ the political," as feminism has done, is to point toward the transformative possibilities of a politics of feminism. But even if such possibilities prove attractive, if the private can be thought identical with the public, then we still may ask whether it will be possible for feminism both to serve personal needs and to sustain its public project of an action-oriented politics directed toward institutional transformation. The alliance between the "political" and the "personal," which appears so promising as a new starting point, may cut in two directions at once: it may indeed illuminate the political content of the self's discontents, but it may also over time inundate the "political" with forces it cannot assimilate, reformulate and redirect. In politics there can be not only too much objectivity of a "realist" sort, as a Machiavelli illustrates, but too much "subjectivity" as well. Feminist political theory may have to choose the kind of political language it is willing to develop and follow. Indeed, the choice of a language is itself likely to become a political issue.

As for political theory, it can only benefit from the questioning of its tradition and assumptions inspired by the new feminisms. It should be open to the possibility of an altered canon and a new political language, whether or not it is one "in which we usually do not believe." The emerging task for a critical feminist political theory will be to make the possible believable, and the believable actual.

Notes

1. For feminist interpretations of these two cases see Susan Moller Okin, "Philosopher Queens and Private Wives—Plato on Women and the Family," *Philosophy and Public Affairs* 6 (1977): 345-69, and the comments on Mill in Carole Pateman, "Feminism and Democracy," in *Democratic Theory and Practice*, ed. Graeme Duncan (Cambridge: Cambridge University Press, 1983), esp. pp. 209-211.

2. For representative critical statements see Jean Bethke Elshtain, "Feminist Discourse and Its Discontents: Language, Power and Meaning," and Jane Marcus, "Storming the Toolshed," in *Feminist Theory, A Critique of Ideology*, ed. Keohane, Rosaldo and Gelpi (Chicago: University of Chicago Press, 1982), pp. 127-145, 217-235.

3. The phrase is Nietzsche's own in *Die fröhliche Wissenschaft (The Gay Science)*, Book 2, sec. 60 (Kaufman translation).

4. *The Prince*, ch. 25 (Ricci translation); this well-known passage is the source of the title for Hanna F. Pitkin, *Fortune is a Woman: Gender and Politics in the Thought of Niccolo Machiavelli* (Berkeley: University of California Press, 1984), the only study of Machiavelli addressed explicitly to the feminist theme.

5. *The Prince*, ch. 17.

6. See Mark Hulliung, *Citizen Machiavelli* (Princeton: Princeton University Press, 1983), p. 120 (and pp. 99-129 generally) for this insufficiently critical view of the raising of Lucrezia's "consciousness."

7. *Faust*, Part I, trans. C.F. MacIntyre (New York: New Directions, 1949), p. 92, lines 2605-2608.

8. These references are to be found in Nietzsche, "Götzen-Dammerung," *Werke*, ed. K. Schlechta, vol.2 (Munich: Hanser, 1955), pp. 1028-1029.

9. "Nietzsche und die Frauen," *Die Zukunft*, no. 25 (24 December 1898): p. 41; Dohm was a leading figure among early German feminists.

10. One example of this tendency is Mary Daly, *Gyn/ecology, The Metaphysics of Radical Feminism* (Boston: Beacon, 1978).

11. One of the earliest philosophical discussions along these lines is between Georg Simmel, "Female Culture" (1911), in *Georg Simmel: On Women, Sexuality, and Love*, trans. Guy Oakes (New Haven: Yale University Press, 1984), pp. 65-101; and Marianne Weber, "Die Frau und die objektive Kultur" (1913), in *Frauenfragen und Frauengedanken, Gesämmelte*

Aufsätze (Tübingen: Mohr, 1919), pp. 95-133. Among feminist utopian writers one of the best examples is still Charlotte Perkins Gilman, *Herland* (New York: Pantheon, 1979), written in 1915.

12. The best representative work is Susan Moller Okin, *Women in Western Political Thought* (Princeton: Princeton University Press, 1981).

13. One example is Jean Bethke Elshtain, *Public Man, Private Woman: Women in Social and Political Thought* (Princeton: Princeton University Press, 1981).

14. For a recent example of the misuses of genetic determinism that constitutes a kind of new "Aristotelianism" see the last chapter of E.O. Wilson, *Sociobiology: The New Synthesis* (Cambridge: Harvard, 1975), and the responses in *The Sociobiology Debate*, ed. A.L. Caplan (New York: Harper, 1978).

15. An excellent example of this kind of theorizing is Catharine A. MacKinnon, "Feminism , Marxism, Method and the State: An Agenda for Theory ," in *Feminist Theory, A Critique of Ideology*, ed. N.O. Keohane et al. (Chicago: University of Chicago Press, 1982), pp. 1-30.

16. Carole Pateman, "Feminism and Democracy," in *Democratic Theory and Practice*, ed. Graeme Duncan (Cambridge: Cambridge University Press, 1983), p. 204.

17. An excellent example of the kind of theorizing I have in mind is Carole Pateman, "The Disorder of Women': Women, Love, and the Sense of Justice," *Ethics* 91 (October 1980): 20-34.

18. G. W.F. Hegel, *Philosophy of Right*, trans. T.M. Knox (London: Oxford, 1952), p. 124 (sec. 185).

19. *Philosophy of Right*, p. 114 (sec. 116).

20. Undoubtedly the most widely-discussed recent defense of woman's moral uniqueness is Carol Gilligan, *In a Different Voice, Psychological Theory and Women's Development* (Cambridge: Harvard, 1982); for an insightful feminist rejoinder see Judy Auerbach et al., "Commentary: On Gilligan's *In a Different Voice*," *Feminist Studies* 11 (Spring 1985): 149-161.

PATRICK O'DONNELL

2. Becoming Discourse:
Eudora Welty's "Petrified Man"

The problem, from the beginning, is language; or rather, more properly, the problem is what happens to language when it becomes "discourse": when it is, in the words of Thomas Pynchon, "taken out of the course flow—shaped, cleaned, rectified, [and] redeemed... from the lawless, mortal streaming of human speech."[1] This is a becoming illusion, for who is to say which came first? Was "lawless" speech there, in the beginning, prior to its redemption under the law of discourse and its conversion into a linguistic system of signs which reveal the pressures of cultural refinement? Or did "language," uttered or inscribed, arise from these very pressures as the signature of our being under the law? What compels us to speak as we do, and what is the source of this compulsion?

The ontological questions posed by looking for the origins of language, while finally unanswerable in any absolute sense, are at least approachable when language as ruled into discourse is considered in light of a feminist critique. Another way of putting this is to remark that one of the crucial functions of some feminist theory is to question the relation of language to culture in several ways.[2] To what extent, for example, is the language we use to speak, write with, and articulate our readings of texts constricted by a repressive cultural order that authorizes patriarchy, materialism, competition without restraint, and unbounded egotism? How much do given political or social realities affect language itself, down to its etymologies and grammatical structures? Does language have the ability, as Bakhtin claims it does when shaped into narrative, to parody the authorized discourse of the day?[3] Or can language be made to work against itself

15

in such a way that, according to Irigaray, it makes visible, "by an effect of playful repetition, what was supposed to remain invisible: the cover-up of a possible operation of the feminine in language"?[4] Can there be a written or spoken language thoroughly "outside" culture, perhaps a women's speech or writing that would incarnate the signs of rupture, otherness, alterity? Finally, wouldn't such a language, if it does or could exist, be powerless, separate, perhaps even unconscious?[5]

More questions; for the question is one of the "proper" forms in which to pose alternatives to a received and appropriate discourse while writing within that discourse. Formulating questions returns us to the proposition that "the problem" has always been language in the first place. We can't critique it without using it. One can't attack the patriarchal structures of culture or the logocentricity of discourse without invoking and repeating them. There is no *other* to this, it seems, at least not in the sense of something completely different, or thoroughly uncanny, or totally unrecognizable. Language, whatever its origin, pressured into whatever discursive forms, might be compared to the light spectrum: we only experience what we see, though we somehow know that there are colors we can't see. But what of the colors we don't know about that we can't see? In this sense, our language seems condemned to its own history, and we to the significations generated by that history.

Yet, despite the assimilatory drive and monolithic pretensions of discourse, to blindly accept our confinement within language in these terms might well be to reinforce those patriarchal structures which threaten to shut out or shut up another language. The strategy of silence is a case in point. Silence by itself, used merely as an alternative to writing or speech (both of which, from a certain view, cannot help but repeat the authoritative, patriarchal structures of discourse), actually reduplicates these, since it allows for a kind of inaudible blank space that can only bear the marks of some other impression. This silence romanticizes the "before" of speech, and its own marginality, as that which is beyond speech while actually becoming its mirrored image. Focusing upon a critique of the origins, boundaries, and negations of discourse in this way can often condemn us to a form of theoretical mimesis whereby, in discussing our seemingly necessary submission to the logocentricity of language, we imitate it. As if, like the picture-drawing ape Nabokov fancifully describes in the afterword to *Lolita*, given the chance to sketch what we see, we draw the bars of our own cage.

There are other ways to think about language, even to think about silence, not as the absolute other of speech, but as something that occurs within speech. Irigaray, for example, sees silence as what occurs between instances of pronunciation, rather than as something that comes before or after language: "What is called for instead is an examination of the *operation of the 'grammar'* of each figure of discourse, its syntactic laws or requirements, its imaginary configurations, its metaphoric networks, and also, of course, what it does not articulate at the level of utterances: *its silences.*"[6] Thus, the power and suggestiveness of an ellipsis as a form of written silence arises from its very placement within the context of writing. In his essay "Differance," Derrida argues for a view of language as a "lawful" system, but one that contains the seeds of its own disorder: "Essentially and lawfully, every concept is inscribed in a chain or in a system within which it refers to the other, to other concepts, by means of the systematic play of differences."[7] Derrida goes on to explain the complex interrelationship between the "system" of language and "difference":

> In a language, in the *system* of language, there are only differences. Therefore a taxonomical operation can undertake the systematic, statistical, and classificatory inventory of a language. But, on the other hand, these differences *play*: in language, in speech too, and in the exchange between language and speech. On the other hand, these differences are themselves *effects*. They have not fallen from the sky fully formed, and are no more inscribed in a *topos noetos*, than they are prescribed in the gray matter of the brain. If the word "history" did not in and of itself convey the motif of a final repression of difference, one could say that only differences can be "historical" from the outset and in each of their aspects.[8]

This is not so much a statement about language as an indication of how we might approach the language that we have, both in understanding its history of differences and in broadening its effects from within.[9] How might this broadening be achieved? How can we induce from the system of language its own alterity—an "otherness" that we may both inscribe within and against the language we use?

Together, Derrida and Irigaray suggest we undertake "a taxonomical operation," and it is just such an operation that I wish to bring to bear on a particular text, Eudora Welty's "Petrified Man." The story itself can be seen as a linguistic system that bears the marks of its own histories and etymologies. These, of course, are not self-contained, since the story is written in a language that is used to tell other stories; what makes the story distinguishable from any other is the unique combination of linguistic signs it manages. On the one hand, "Petrified Man" is "just another story"; on the other hand, it relates the singular history of its own linguistic being. If we can uncover this history, by paying close attention to the story's etymologies and the discursive orders by which it imitates some view or other of a larger "reality," then we may be able to see the story itself as a "difference" amidst those stories Welty wishes to evoke in her "regionalist" tale of life in the beauty parlor. Approached in this way, I shall argue that "Petrified Man" imitates, and parodies by imitation, a language which is comically patriarchal. Welty mimes the discourse she is constrained to write within, but this mimicry, by its very imitation of a language of mastery, sounds a voice that echoes with the irony and laughter which accompanies the vision of crumbling idols. The issues of "Petrified Man"—authority, imitation, and durability—speak to the conditions of a received narrative discourse. Welty, simply, creates a voice (that of the narrator) which describes these conditions, and which, by the parodic manipulation of the story's language, breaks them down. *That* voice, I wish to argue, arranges it so that we are exposed to the dead ends of one language, and the becoming disguises of another.

"Petrified Man" is ostensibly a series of gossipy conversations that take place between a beautician, Leota, and her customer, Mrs. Fletcher. The two women discuss their husbands, sex lives, pregnancies, the "new girl" in town, and the attractions of a travelling carnival—all within the grotesque confines of a beauty parlor described as "a den of curling fluid and henna packs," where supposedly henpecking women are "gratified," "cooked," and wound up into "spirals."[10] It would be possible to read "Petrified Man" within a canonically-defined historical context by regarding it as a fragment of local color realism set in the American South of, roughly, the 1930s. Indeed, the story has generally been viewed in this light, and the tendency of such a reading is to foreground Welty's satire as she depicts the activities and gossip to be found in a typical beauty parlor of the Deep South. Similar to most works which can be categorized as examples of local color or regionalism, the point of the satire in "Petrified Man" is to show the peculiarities and limitations of a certain group of people (in this case, lower-middle class women) who inhabit a certain landscape (small Southern city), speak a noticeable dialect (Mississippi, gossip), and share a common history (here, a history of displacement and marital conflict typical of twentieth-century citified, but undereducated, women of this class and locale). Similar to the Mrs. Todd of Sarah Orne Jewett's *The Country of the Pointed Firs*, or the home-bound draftee of Hamlin Garland's "The Return of the Private," the conversationalists of "Petrified Man" seem to be semiallegorical "types" who signify a sociology of character and culture. If the reactions of my students are any indication—even those who have never been to the South and who know the American "1930s" only as something (possibly) in their parents' memory—Leota and Mrs. Fletcher are quite recognizable as the kind of people who would frequent beauty parlors then, and who continue to do so now. True, the story makes use of hyperbole and classical allusion—particularly to the myth of the Medusa—but only, in the view of a "canonical" reading, to point out the wrenched inconsistencies and demeaned aspects of small-town contemporary life. That is, even those readers for whom the cultural context has shifted dramatically from the setting represented in Welty's story, Leota and Mrs. Fletcher are identifiable stereotypes.[11]

In this view, then, the story is "realistic." It gives us a "real," though exaggerated feeling for the times Welty was writing about, the kinds of characters one might have encountered in the South during that time, what one might have "really" overheard had she been in the next booth at the beauty parlor. The tone and topics of Leota's and Mrs. Fletcher's conversations fall quite easily within expectations established by a story that considers the types Leota and Mrs. Fletcher represent. When Mrs. Fletcher expresses anxiety about the fact that anyone might notice her recent pregnancy, Leota responds: " 'Well, now, honey, I just want you to know—I habm't told any of my ladies and I ain't goin' to tell 'em—even that you're losin' your hair. You just get one of those Stork-a-Lure dresses and stop worryin': What people don't know don't hurt nobody, as Mrs. Pike says.' " (19). Leota's dialect and the reference to "Stork-a-Lure" dresses tells us what this story is about within the reading parameters of "local color" realism. Here, women feed off and nourish each other's anxieties; here, the cultural code and the torture chamber atmosphere of the beauty parlor reflect a conception of beauty as artificial, antinatural; here, the seductive power of women (the "allure") is viewed as the precedent to marriage—a power that is satirized when it is carried over to the visible results of marriage.

Several interpretive generalizations issue from a reading of the story's particularities of dialect, conversational subject, and local grotesquerie—the latter hilariously represented by the spectacle of a travelling freak show and its main attraction, the fake petrified man. By carefully depicting the "realistic" speech patterns and "typical" concerns of these two women within the parodic confines of the beauty parlor-cum-inferno, Welty satirizes Southern habits, middle-class marriage, and modern corporal aesthetics. More broadly, she satirizes women, or at least those "kinds" of women whom one might well find in less surreal beauty parlors, yesterday and today. Thus, "Petrified Man" is a story of manners and a humorous rendition of gossip overheard by a narrator whose irony affords us both information about these local characters and insight about our own circumstances, however far removed they may be from those of the story. The popularity and persuasive power of such a reading can be explained by noting that it, on the one hand, reinforces the generic category to which the story is consigned (that of local color realism) while, on the other hand, promulgating a satiric view of women that matches certain cultural stereotypes. Within this reading, the story is both a satirical "sketch" (thus, not a major work) and, in some way, a representation of women *as they are* in such places as beauty parlors. Thus addressed, "Petrified Man" is both disabling and disabled generically and substantively. While these characters, since they mirror a certain "minor" segment of culture over which most readers would assume a certain intellectual and experiential superiority, are not to be taken seriously, the views of sex, marriage, and women that emerge from their conversations are to be taken as *representative* in some way. To put it more bluntly, read this way within a patriarchal view of language and culture, "Petrified Man" proclaims its own parochialism while incorporating a more general view of women as backbiting, unintelligent, artificial creatures who reign over the equally stereotypical, henpecked men of the story. More largely then, modern, fallen "human nature" is satirized in "Petrified Man" for its inherent meanness, stupidity, and humor—but, notably, a human nature that is represented through the language of women.[12]

Another reading of "Petrified Man," one which stands as a form of mirrored opposition to the canonical reading I've just proposed, might be crudely entitled a "thematized feminist" interpretation. Thematization of literary texts is manifested in nearly every critical approach which assumes that there must be a reflective connection between the text and the reality the approach attempts to describe. Thus, some Marxist critics will scan literary texts for evidence of superstructure and class conflict, as will some Freudian critics pursue the schematization of Freud's metapsychology in the plot and scene of a story. There are a number of compelling reasons to assume that the language of a text reflects a structure of reality that may adequately describe some elements of the larger reality, or world, to which a text belongs. All too often, however, the thematizing critic assumes that the language of literary texts enacts a simple *representational* function, a notion which language itself throws into question. While a thematized feminist reading of "Petrified Man" may raise crucial issues and genuinely attempt to reverse the assumptions of a canonical reading, it, like the canonical reading, in some way glosses over the interior history of the textual language itself. Instead it tries to place the interpreter in a static position outside that language.

Such a reading might begin with the notion of "women's space," and approach the scene of "Petrified Man" as an enactment of that space.[13] There is much in the story to encourage this. The beauty parlor, after all, might be seen as a separated area where women are allowed to act out their power struggles and desires. As Leota and Mrs. Fletcher discuss the latter's boarder, Mrs. Pike, they reveal the actual or imaginary power they have over men. Mrs. Fletcher says of any resistance her husband might offer, " 'If he so much as raises his voice against me, he knows good and well I'll have one of my sick headaches, and then I'm just not fit to live with' " (19). Leota relates her formidable seductive power as she tells Mrs. Fletcher about her first date with her future husband: " 'Honey, me an' Fred, we met in a rumble seat eight months ago and we was practically on what you might call the way to the altar inside of half an hour' " (23). Babies and husbands must wait on the strong-willed Mrs. Montjoy, who somehow manages to withstand labor pains while beautifying herself for her stay at the hospital: " 'See, her husband was waitin' outside in the car, and her bags was all packed an' in the back seat, an' she was all ready, 'cept she wanted her shampoo an' set. An' havin' one pain right after another. Her

husband kep' comin' in here, scared-like, but couldn't do nothin'
with her a course. She yelled bloody murder, too, but she always
yelled her head off when I give her a perm'nent' " (24). The petrified
man, who is undone by Mrs. Pike, can be viewed as a demeaned
everyman who is put in his place by Mrs. Pike's perceptive powers
which, Medusa-like, fix him in place while revealing the fraudulency
of "a man made of stone." Her castrative power, a remarkable
reversal of penis envy, is transfused to all the women in the beauty
parlor in the story's final scene, where "Billy Boy" ("billy club"?),
the child who is the potential father to the story's men, is comically,
symbolically victimized and cast out by the laughing women. True,
these events take place under the gaze of Welty's satirical eye, which
envisages the pathetic nature of these power plays. But at the same
time, the story has successfully generated a space where the potential
power of women, however parodically, has been expressed, and
where the potency of "the male world" is drained off and ridiculed.
In this reading, Leota, particularly, emerges as an embodiment of
sexual power who, in the present context, misuses her authority, but
who has the potential to transform (as she beautifies) her world.

In many ways, this thematic reading is attractive, even as it
ignores much of the story's tone, for it attempts to pierce through
social satire to get at the real, operative sources of desire and power
in Welty's world. It also confronts the canonical reading by referring
to the deeper, more ambiguous sources in myth the story taps.
Strangely, however, the thematic reading in some ways reinforces the
canonical reading by assuming the normative characteristics of the
story's language and promoting the allegorized realism of its effects.
In short, both readings regard the story as primarily descriptive,
either of Southern life or of women's space, which is to regard the
language of the fiction itself as, somehow, mirroring, reflective of the
"reality" it defines or prescribes. This is to view language, in general,
as a representational medium. It is directly against a representational
conception of language, on the contrary, that the story works as it
evolves its own language. By creating a language that reduplicates,
while parodying, the operations of the received, authorized discourse of a "male" reality, "Petrified Man" reconsiders and mocks,
linguistically, the issues of genealogy, representation, and power that
it thematically or canonically represents. Welty's story makes fun of
itself. In Irigaray's terms, it performs a "mimicry" of itself, it "plays"
with mimesis; in Cixous' punning phraseology, it "breaks up" the

"truth" or "realism" of a masculine discourse with laughter—but a laughter echoed by the language of the text, rather than represented by the plot of the story.[14] In so doing, "Petrified Man" reveals both the power of language to underwrite "reality" and its powerlessness in the face of its own radical ambivalence and ironic etymology.

I have spent some time on two possible readings of "Petrified Man" because the third which now ensues properly has its beginnings in the first two. It uses, while it departs from, the revelations generated by a canonical and thematic reading of the text, just as it relies on a representational theory of language in order to counter that theory. The etymological reading I propose initially takes words as signs and signs as elements in an informal language system generated both by the story and the history of the language. We might consider the story a type of "word-hoard" or, as Derrida suggested earlier of all language, an unwieldy, mutable collection of differences. The story's title is telling in this regard: not "The Petrified Man" or "A Petrified Man," but an unarticled "Petrified Man," as if we were about to read a scientific treatise on a new species of *homo sapiens* which would trace the genesis and history of its subject. The title playfully allows us to consider the language of "Petrified Man" as naming its genealogy and tracing its own linguistic history.

This genealogy, I wish to suggest, occurs within a larger etymology intimated by the themes and keywords of "Petrified Man"—an etymology that reflects the patriarchal discourse which the story mimes and mocks. To illustrate, I offer the following "word family" as an explanatory device which illuminates the story's underlying linguistic strategies *(See illustration on following page)*. Reading the etymology from top to bottom suggests a movement between the discourse of the father and that of the mother; in terms of the story, this illusory "progression" is really cyclical, a post-meridian return of *pater* disguised as *mater*. But the place to begin a scrutiny of this etymology as it arises from both the language of the story and the history of the English language is in the middle, with the word "petrify," which labels the grotesque subject of the women's discourse in "Petrified Man." From this vantage point, we can look "up" to the authoritative source of the word "petrify" and the language to which it belongs, as well as "down" to its dissemination as its meanings and implications divide and multiply. Thus, the language of the story, seen through this graph, both returns

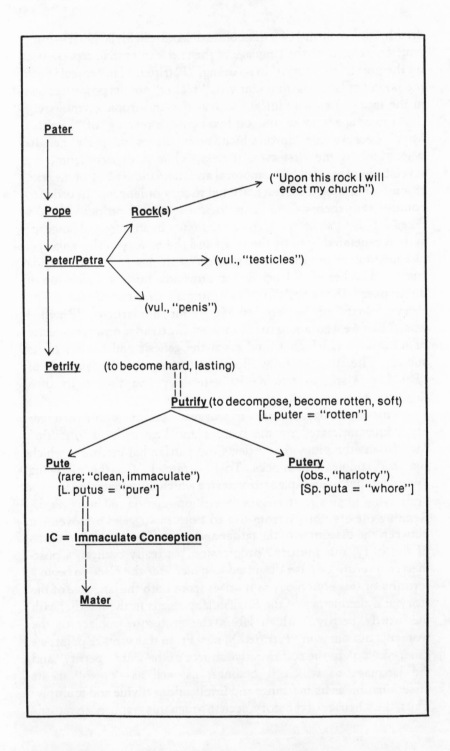

upon itself and "de"-generates, a paradox which, I shall argue, reflects the essential, peculiar power of Welty's fictional discourse.

"To petrify" means "to become hard," though infrequently the verb may be used in its transitive sense of "to make hard," as in "she petrified me with her glance." Petrification, the process by which something is hardened, may be applied in a normative sense to an object, like a tree, which has metamorphosed into a form that will endure. More ironically, petrification can refer to something which was once living, organic, and is now dead, inorganic. Given the explicit sexual content of Welty's story, which deals with impotent, henpecked husbands and domineering wives, as well as with the "actual" petrified man, the process of petrification accrues to itself several seemingly contradictory senses. The hardness of the petrified man, whose real name is Mr. Petrie, is a fake durability. The soft food he chews which supposedly "goes to his joints" and turns to stone by means of his unique digestive processes, really goes to his stomach, leaving those "joints" as bony and brittle as those of any "old bird" who, according to Leota, " 'musta had one foot in the grave, at least' " (27). By means of the cosmetic white powder he wears all over his body, the petrified man appears to "be hard" but he isn't; to Leota and Mrs. Fletcher, he is a source of fetishistic fascination until his true identity is revealed, whereupon he becomes a sign of old age and impotence. The fact that he raped four women as the putative Mr. Petrie assumes the guise of a grim joke, hardly attributable to the old bird on the verge of death. Here, Leota speaks first:

> "Four women. I guess those women didn't have the faintest notion at the time they'd be worth a hundred an' twenty-five bucks apiece some day to Mrs. Pike. We ast her how old the fella was then, an' she says he musta had one foot in the grave, at least. Can you beat it?"
>
> "Not really petrified at all, of course," said Mrs. Fletcher meditatively. She drew herself up. "I'd 'a' felt something," she said proudly.
>
> "Shoot! I did feel somethin'," said Leota. "I tole Fred when I got home I felt so funny. I said, 'Fred, that ole petrified man sure did leave me with a funny feelin'.' He says, 'Funny-haha or funny-peculiar?' and I says, 'Funny-peculiar.' " She pointed her comb into the air emphatically.
>
> I'll bet you did," said Mrs. Fletcher. (27-28)

As a joke upon four innocent women, or as an image of the
defused uncanny ("funny-peculiar"), Petrie's power as seductive
object (even as a potential object of so-called "rape fantasies") is
effectively undermined. His hardness is softened; his ability to "keep
it up" (his disguise) is revealed as a matter of the powder puff; his
endurance is transformed into the sign of his impending death. Like
the pygmies in the travelling freak show, he becomes in the eyes of
the women one of "the teeniniest men in the universe" (21).

Clearly, the associations surrounding Petrie's false petrification
formulate a satire upon certain "male" sexual fantasies involving the
hardness and lastingness of phallic power; the women, in the end,
could be seen as disabusing themselves of this power by unmasking
the petrified man and by comically scapegoating Petrie's juvenile
stand-in, Billy Boy. Certainly the conception of their husbands as
unemployed layabouts (Leota's Fred "lay[s] around the house like
a rug" [22]), or Sunday fishermen who catch no fish reinforces a
view of the story as a send-up of male potency. Yet the beauty parlor,
in its entirety, might be seen as a redramatization, rather than casting
out of this power. The process of beautification is imaged as a process
of petrification where women turn that eternal sign of feminine
potency and seductiveness—their hair—into stone. These women,
literally, make themselves *up* as they transform themselves into the
specular objects of the male gaze doubled in the mirrors which the
women use to view themselves. One woman is "half wound for a
spiral"; another is enduring the delights of a "machineless"; Mrs.
Fletcher reminds Leota not to "cook" her for too long; all are getting
"permanents" (18). Indeed, the power of the Medusa is invoked as
Leota "drench[es] Mrs. Fletcher's hair with a thick fluid and
catch[es] the overflow in a cold wet towel at her neck" (18), but, in
context, the curling of Mrs. Fletcher's hair hardly seems a "powerful" sign of her transformation into gorgon. The "den" of beauty is,
naturally, replete with mirrors, and it is in this realm of reflection
that the women experience various forms of "gratification" which
appear as violent replications of Petrie's rapes. Leota presses into
Mrs. Fletcher's scalp "with strong red-nailed fingers" (17); Mrs.
Fletcher's falling hair "float[s] out of the lavender teeth" of Leota's
comb" (17); another beautician, Thelma, vampirishly "droop[s] her
blood-red lips and look[s] over Mrs. Fletcher's head into the
mirror" (18); Billy Boy is often "slapped brightly" and suffers a
communal spanking, while Leota views the raped women as

prostitutes when she figures how much each is "worth" in terms of the reward money. In short, the gratification being offered in the beauty parlor is a mirror reflection of the "gratification" offered by male rape fantasies and power plays. Playing Medusa, the women in fact "re-play" Mr. Petrie; in their actions, they reduplicate that which they symbolically castrate and, in so doing, castrate themselves. Like Petrie, the beauty parlor is a fraud: it postulates itself as an arena of beautiful transformations, but its effects are purely cosmetic. Such is the power of reflection in Welty's story that it comically takes in everything, as these women "become" the men they satirize and dominate.[15]

If we place "petrify" within the larger context of the linguistic genealogy from which it descends and which it reflects, we discover the cultural weightiness of the keyword Welty chooses to name her story. According to the OED, "petrify" comes from the Latin *petra* and the Greek *petros*, meaning "rock" or "stone." The name, "Peter," is related to this noun; thus, the declaration of Jesus to the disciples in Matthew 16:18—"So now I say to you: You are Peter and on this rock I will build my Church"—punningly names the disciple Peter as both the enduring foundation and head, or first pope of Christendom.[16] The word "pope" comes from the Latin *papa* and is related to the word for "father," *pater*. This etymology might be called the "sacred ascent" of "Peter" to "Pater"; however, the word cluster "petrify-peter-pope-pater" retains a series of more profane associations, particularly when it is placed within the framework of Welty's worldly discourse of the father. For, within the realm of assumed male fantasies, to become "hard" or "petrified," and to endure in this state, is a sign of potency. To be or have a "peter," a petrified penis, is also to be or have "rocks," testicles, which testify to one's status as a living erection. These vulgarisms can be seen as placed within a "pater-nal" taxonomy, so that by a slight shift in vision, the sacred etymology becomes a sexual alignment where fantasies of size, endurance, and potency are verbally played out.

"Petrified Man" dwells within this second taxonomy by virtue of the fact that the women in the story reenact these fantasies in their own discourse. They view the petrified man as a source of fascination precisely because his "petrification" symbolically satisfies the "male" desires they are condemned to by virtue of their entrance into a symbolic order that constructs desire in "male" terms. Such desires are partially fulfilled through the Medusizing and rivalrous

violence of the beauty parlor. When Petrie proves false, their comic
dismay at the displacement and inauthenticity of his "power" is
taken out on each other and the male child/pygmy, Billy Boy.
Thoroughly socialized within the parameters of a patriarchal "reality," the women place themselves and are placed under the rubric of
this vulgar discourse, where they "find" their language and identity.
What they may not see is that the other side of this discourse signifies
impotency and death. Trees, twigs, and other phallic objects which
petrify—even hair—must die or be denatured; the pressured
anxieties underlying the "peter-pater" etymology regarding the
potency and largesse of the phallus reveal the enduring fear of
impotency, pygmyism, or "billy-boyism."

Thus, in a show of power, Bill Boy is cast out of the beauty
parlor at the end, but not without a defiant parting shot: " 'If you're
so smart, why ain't you rich?' " (28). The "boy" or son who would
be a man and who, at the same time, represents an undesirable
version of "unmanliness" as he hangs around the beauty parlor, is
oedipally victimized by the "manly" women at the end. His words,
however, which are the last of the story, strike at the heart of the
anxieties that found this comic, tortured scene, for as Leota has
formerly remarked, the worth of women is viewed here in strictly
economic terms. The victims of Petrie's rapes are worth so much as
objects of exchange in this paternal system. Billy Boy's remark serves
the double purpose of devaluing the women in the beauty parlor as
"women" while remarking on their impotency as "men" who are
unable to thoroughly silence their victim, exchange other women for
money (since Mrs. Pike, not Leota, gets the reward), or retain the
now "rich" Mrs. Pike as a neighbor and object of conversation. In
effect, the beauty parlor becomes the mirrored representation of
male discourse and male fantasies as imaged forth by the language of
petrification, which has its roots in the language of paternity. The
phallic nature of such language, Irigaray suggests, is "hard" and
systematic when compared to a potential "writing of women" which
is "never fixed in the possible identity-to-self of some form or other.
It is always *fluid* ... [it] resists and explodes every firmly established
form, figure, idea, or concept."[17] Thus, these women do business in
the name of the father and, rather than subverting the signs of his
authority or "improperly" overtaking it (i.e., as women who are, in
an unauthorized fashion, acting like men) they simply repeat these
signs in their own language. In so doing, they victimize themselves

while reduplicating the vulgarities of a "petriarchal" discourse.

If we allow for a slight play of differences in this discourse we may see one place where it leads. The anxiety aroused by an obsession with potency often leads to impotency, as hard leads to soft, as petrify leads to its opposite, putrify. Becoming "soft" in "Petrified Man" is exactly what the women in the story wish to avoid as they harden their hair and their hearts, or as they express dismay over Mrs. Fletcher's pregnancy. She fears that her body will become soft, flatulent; she wishes to disguise that ripeness which signifies to her a form of decomposition, a ripeness leading to rottenness. The word "putrify" represents the senses of these anxieties in its descent from the Latin *puter*, which means "rotten." In the sexual dialectic which the story proposes, to "putrify" (to be pregnant) carries with it the double threat of becoming soft, old, and in some paradoxical sense, impotent though fertile, as well as becoming part of a different and demeaned sign system, that of the mother. The dual sense of the word is revealed in Leota's comment on Mrs. Fletcher's pregnancy: " 'I don't mean to insist or insinuate or anything, Mrs. Fletcher, but Thelma's lady just happ'med to throw out—I forgotten what she was talkin' about at the time—that you was p-r-e-g., and lots of times that'll make your hair do awful funny, fall out and God knows what all. It just ain't our fault, is the way I look at it' " (18). Here, pregnancy leads to guilt and impotence (Mrs. Fletcher's hair falling out), a punishment for femaleness that the strong-willed Mrs. Montjoy gets a last-minute permanent to avoid, despite her labor pains and Leota's sadism. So intense is the anxiety the powerful, taboo word arouses in these women that Leota won't even pronounce it as she speaks to Mr. Fletcher in hushed tones. No one wants to admit that this form of "putrification" can insinuate itself into this codified world of petrification.

Interestingly, we can see derivations of "putrify" that take us in opposite directions as "degenerations" of the paternal taxonomy. On one side, the obsolete English word "putery" descends from the Latin *puter*, and means "harlotry" or "whoredom." A more familiar and still-used form of this is the Spanish *puta*, "whore." On the other side, there is the English "pute," a word in rare usage which means "clean" or "immaculate"; it descends from the Latin *putus*, meaning "pure," which is the antonym of *puter* though both words appear to have the same etymological root. In these declensions, we see a "word-family" carrying on a civil war as the sign (in Welty's story) for woman splits off into its two stereotyped senses: prostitute and virgin. Indeed, the story can be seen to support these senses in the eyes of the women themselves when we recall, for example, that Petrie's rape victims are read as exchange objects ("whores"). In similar ways, recalling Mrs. Fletcher's headaches and Leota's productive ride in a rumble seat, we can see that virginity or sexual abstinence is "worth" something in the world of the beauty parlor: it is the price of admission for entrance into the realm of a dominant male power. That is, the women of the story signify themselves as "coin of the realm" in order to enter into the taxonomy of paternal coinages so that they may have some measure of power within that economy. Of course, this form of negative power can only be viewed ironically: while it is itself "illicit" and corrupt, it offers a way for the story's women to retain some unofficial, *ad hoc* control in a world where women are legally powerless.

Another way of putting this is to say that the women submit their language (i.e., "gossip") to an etymological history and authority that condemns them to mere repetition of a discourse which marks women as virgins and whores. It's a leap (but not such a great one, given the concern with virginity and pregnancy in "Petrified Man") from "pute," meaning "immaculate," to "IC," the acronym for the "Immaculate Conception" of the Virgin Mary. We might say that the conception of her is "male," that as a "holy, great mother" or *mater*, she fits into the scheme of things. Thus, a symbol of potentially enormous weight and power, a "discourse of the mother," comes under the law of and reflects the paternal discourse, just as Leota's and Mrs. Fletcher's attitudes towards pregnancy reinforce the fantasies of petrification which "get women that way" in the first place.[18] The senses to be associated with the Immaculate Conception (which involves the birth of Mary without original sin, *not* the birth of Christ) may seem far from the concerns of the beauty parlor. But then this "conception" is, theoretically, one of the ends of the pater-nal taxonomy, the furthest extension of one of its fantasies regarding women, where the undesired "putrification" of pregnancy is purified by the notion that the female container of divine power is timeless, permanent, unstained by birth and sexuality, impregnated by the power of a Word. Ultimately, words rule in this realm of Southern beautification, as they do in a discourse that, moving between the differences of "pater-peter-puter-mater," reproduces itself at every point. Here, as surely as a multitude of mirrors reflects their petrified heads, the speech of women reflects and repeats the strictures of a fatherly discourse subjecting maternity to itself: *mater* becomes *pater*; "male" and "female" are wound up, like the women's petrified hair, into a discursive spiral that, eternally, circles back on itself.

I have been insisting on the reflective tendencies of language in Welty's story because it is those tendencies she both imitates and parodies, as she does the story's informing myth of the Medusa. Potentially, as Cixous argues, the Medusa is a symbol of great subversive power as she petrifies men with a glance, but when she is "placed" within the kind of reflective taxonomy at work within "Petrified Man," her power is cut off.[19] When Perseus wishes to kill her, knowing that he may not look at her directly, he uses his highly-polished shield to mirror her image so that, by this reflection, he may decapitate her. Thus through mimesis is Medusa slain, just as the women's imitation of a male discourse in "Petrified Man," in effect, slays them as they are anchored into the discursive system which their language replicates. If there is a real Medusa in the story, it would appear to be Petrie, whom the women gaze upon with fixed, fascinated stares—but of course his Medusal qualities are inverted: he is male; he petrifies himself (falsely) rather than others, though he, like the Medusa of myth, is undone by a reflection when Mrs. Pike recognizes his face in a photograph. As for the "heads" in the beauty shop, they, too, are self-petrified in unceasing permanents while they speak a language that has hardened into the unbecoming speech patterns of a reflected "capital" discourse.

It may sound as if Welty ends up where I began this discussion: with a negative answer to the question of whether or not there is another language that counters the received language of the day. In "Petrified Man," a realm of potential alterity (the beauty parlor) is merely a repetition of the same. Even the taxonomical system of linguistic differences that I have pursued through the story seems to result in a repetitious, circular discourse where women become the spokespersons for acculturated male fantasies and significations of women. Yet it is equally possible that Welty effects an unknotting of these linguistic binds precisely through a form of disfiguring mimesis. By imitating a set of stereotyped speech patterns (these are the "kinds of things" women talk about while having their hair done) and placing these within the ludicrous context offered by the local color grotesquerie of "Petrified Man," Welty parodies the taxonomy and effects of a pater-nal discourse. In a sense, she uses reflection against itself as she subjects the language of her own story to the ridicule of the ironic narrative voice that tells it.

Where does this voice come from, and how is it presented when what we have on the page largely appears to be the transcription of two dialogues between Leota and Mrs. Fletcher? Bakhtin gives us a clue when he defines the rise of the novel as signifying the emergence of European civilization "from a socially isolated and culturally deaf semipatriarchal society, and its entrance into international and interlingual contacts and relationships."[20] For Bakhtin, "novel" is a linguistic phenomenon which disrupts the received discourses of Western culture; "novelization" results in a loosening of generic bonds: "They become more free and flexible, their language renews itself by incorporating extraliterary heteroglossia and the 'novelistic' layers of literary language, they become dialogized, permeated with laughter, irony, humor, elements of self-parody and finally—this is the most important thing—the novel inserts into these other genres an indeterminacy, a certain semantic open-endedness, a living contact with the unfinished, still-evolving contemporary reality (the open-ended present)."[21] Bakhtin's formalistic dialogism can lead to Cixous' more radical sense of "laughter" in the feminine text which is "volcanic; as it is written it brings about an upheaval of the old property crust, carrier of masculine investments; there's no other way. There's no room for her if she's not a he. If she's a her-she, it's in order to smash everything, to shatter the framework of institutions, to blow up the law, to break up the 'truth' with laughter".[22] It is this sense of "novel" and "laughter" that "Petrified Man" expresses as it destructively imitates the sexual (rather than "generic") codes it means to parody.

For the fact of the matter is that Leota and Mrs. Fletcher are talking to each other, and though they do so within the "generic" confines of a male discourse, their speech goes on. In the funny, *ad hoc*, dialogic potential of speech itself we can hear the faint echoes of a response to the story's hardened patterns of discourse; we hear the echo more strongly when Billy Boy, in the story's final speech, flings back his rejoinder to the women who have scapegoated him. We hear parody in Welty's imitation of Leota's Southern dialect, her "habm'ts" and "honey's" and "I declare's" which are stereotypes of so-called local color speech, as well as bastardizations of any official, authorized American dialect. We hear the intonations of mockery in the confused discursive patterns of the story itself, which mixes Mississippi dialect and Greek myth, the low-brow comedy of popular culture (Stork-a-lure dresses and Jax beer) with the high-tone literariness conveyed by the story's allusiveness, or its heavy consonances ("Mrs. Fletcher gladly reached over the lavender shelf under the lavender-framed mirror, shook a hair net loose from the clasp of the patent-leather bag, and slapped her hand down quickly on a powder puff which burst out when the purse was opened" [17]). Within the repetitions of a paternal discourse, we see comically ineffectual role reversals which parody the conception of "role" itself as Petrie is transformed into a male Medusa while the barbering Leota becomes a female Perseus (and yet, still a Medusa) who petrifies her customers. These imitations, dissonances, and reversals originate in the narrative "voice" that transcribes the women's conversations while, interlinearally, even alphabetically ridiculing them. The voice of mockery breaks up, and breaks down the petrified discourse of Welty's story; it offers, from within, an otherness which, in Bakhtin's conception, "dialogizes" the language of the story. This voice, for Irigaray, disrupts the "domination of the philosophic logos [that] stems in larger part from its power to *reduce all others to the economy of the Same*"—a logos whose primary function is "to reduplicate itself, to reflect itself by itself."[23] Welty's self-parody (the mocking of her own language as short story writer and local colorist) not only disrupts the paternal discourse "Petrified Man" so well reflects, it renews language and gives life to its own petrifications. For this disruption caused by the sound of authorial laughter is the source of the story's indeterminacies, its questioning of its own language, origin, and ends. Welty thus breathes life into this story, as she brings to its speech the ironies and importations of a replicative linguistic history and the observances of speech in "everyday life."

To return at last to the question of an alternative language to that ruled by a paternalistic discourse: "Petrified Man" offers one response to speech and language dominated by a history of repetitions and reflections—an alternative where, for Derrida (with qualifications), difference, for Cixous, laughter, and for Irigaray, "fluidity" formulate outworkings from this discourse. The power of Welty's story lies precisely in its ability to represent a language which it escapes through the faithfulness of its execution and its parodic subversions. It is worth noting that these movements take place in a

fiction, where any alternative languages must necessarily be subjected to the rule of mimesis, if only, eventually, to overturn it.
Indeed, there may be other, more radically violent disruptions of an
authorized discourse which, I have been arguing, engages in mirroring while regenerating itself. There remain silence and some kinds of
poetry, the languages of so-called schizophrenia and the languages we
do not yet know. Still, the response elicited by a hearing of "Petrified
Man" may be one of the most effective we have at present, if only for
the moment. In Welty's story, the mode of knowing and speaking we
call "representation," which is at the foundation of our language as it
is at the bottom of our anxieties regarding our becoming identities, is
made to represent its own limits and suicidal tendencies. So, as in
the final line of the story, there is no last word to this—only the
sound of an authorial laughter that questions the necessities of
fiction and the ways of speech. The novel's final line is, again, spoken
by "the little man" having the self-mocking "last word." Billy Boy's
repartee, " 'If you're so smart, why ain't you rich?' " comes back to
the reader as it lays open questions regarding our understanding of
what we've read, or our ability to economize the interpretive riches
the text offers.[24] We will not be allowed to patronize this story, nor
will we be able to petrify its meanings, however we might want to
represent them.

Notes

1. Thomas Pynchon, *Gravity's Rainbow* (New York: Viking, 1973), p. 355.

2. The undecidable issue of the relation of language to culture is, indeed, one of the primary concerns of feminist theory, for upon it hinges the possibilities of "women's writing." The basis for my discussion of this relation in "Petrified Man" relies on two crucial works of feminist theory: Hélène Cixous, "The Laugh of the Medusa," trans. Paula Cohen and Keith Cohen, *Signs* 1 (1976): 875-98; and Luce Irigaray, "The Power of Discourse and the Subordination of the Feminine," in *This Sex Which Is Not One*, trans. Catherine Porter (Ithaca: Cornell University Press, 1985), pp. 65-85. I shall refer to these explicitly within the context provided by the critical work done on the issues of women and language provided by several essays in three critical anthologies. These include, in *New French Feminisms*, ed. Elaine Marks and Isabelle de Courtivon (New York: Schocken Books, 1978): Hélène Cixous, "Sorties" (pp. 90-98), Xaviere Gautier, "Is There Such a Thing as Women's Writing?" (pp. 161-64), Marguerite Duras, "From an Interview" (pp. 174-76), and Claudine Hermann, "Women in Space and Time" (pp. 168-73); in *The Future of Difference*, ed. Hester Eisenstein and Alice Jardine (Boston: G.K. Hall & Co., 1980): Domna C. Stanton, "Language and Revolution: The Franco-American Dis-Connection" (pp. 73-87), Rachel Blau du Plessis and Members of Workshop 9, "For the Etruscans: Sexual Difference and Artistic Production—The Debate Over a Female Aesthetic" (pp. 128-156), and Naomi Schor, "For a Restricted Thematics: Writing, Speech, and Difference in *Madame Bovary*" (pp. 167-85); in *Women and Language in Literature and Society*, ed. Sally McConnell-Ginet, Ruth Borker, and Nelly Furman (New York: Praeger, 1980): Nelly Furman, "Textual Feminism" (pp. 45-54), Josephine Donovan, "The Silence is Broken" (pp. 205-218), Peggy Kamuf, "Writing Like a Woman" (pp. 284-99), and Caren Greenberg, "Reading Reading: Echo's Abduction of Language" (pp. 300-309).

3. Mikhail Bakhtin, *The Dialogic Imagination: Four Essays*, trans. Caryl Emerson and Michael Holquist (Austin: University of Texas Press, 1981), pp. 5-7; 59-60.

4. Irigaray, "The Power of Discourse," p. 76.

5. See Josette Feral, "Antigone or the Irony of the Tribe," *Diacritics* 9 (1978): 2-14, for a discussion of this last point via Kristeva and Irigaray within a Lacanian context. Feral writes that, within an unrevised Freudian metaphysics, "The woman is an Unconscious, she is the other, 'the desire for the other,' that is to say, everywhere and nowhere" (4).

6. Irigaray, "The Power of Discourse," p. 76.

7. Jacques Derrida, "Differance," in *Margins of Philosophy*, trans. Alan Bass (Chicago: University of Chicago Press, 1982), p. 11.

8. Ibid., p.11.

9. But see Gayatri Spivak, "Displacement and the Discourse of Women" in *Displacement: Derrida and After* (Bloomington: Indiana University Press, 1983), pp. 169-95. Spivak argues that Derrida's notions of difference, otherness, and play in passages like these are really forms of disguised androcentrism, and that his promotion of "the undecidability factor" in language is actually a form of powerlessness relegated to "feminine writing" and woman-as-subject.

10. Eudora Welty, "Petrified Man," in *The Collected Stories of Eudora Welty* (New York: Harcourt, Brace, Jovanovich, 1980), p. 17. All references will be to this edition and will be noted parenthetically in the text. "Petrified Man" was originally published in 1941 in *A Curtain of Green and Other Stories*.

11. For interpretations of "Petrified Man" which, despite some considerable variations, pursue what I am defining as the canonical line here and below, see Elizabeth Evans, *Eudora Welty* (New York: Ungar, 1981), p. 40 (though Evans disagrees that the story's characters are stereotypes but, instead, sees them as authentic originals in the tradition of American humor); Ruth M. Vande Kieft, *Eudora Welty* (Boston: Twayne, 1962), pp. 72-75; Alfred Appel, *A Season of Dreams: The Fiction of Eudora Welty* (Baton Rouge: Louisiana State University Press, 1965), pp. 91-99; and Michael Kreyling, *Eudora Welty's Achievement of Order* (Baton Rouge: Louisiana State University Press, 1980), pp. 8-9. Appel focuses on the use of the grotesque in Welty's fiction, arguing that the "petrified man symbolizes all the ultimately destructive possibilities of a life between the sexes that has been distorted by grossness of spirit" (98). Kreyling argues that the grotesquerie and local color of Welty's early stories, including "Petrified Man," reveal in terms of technique a larger order which is "beyond the maker...in the world, to be reached for" (6). As I indicate below, this universalizing of the story is complicit with its categorization as a bit of satirical "local color" which, allegorically, speaks to the larger tendencies of "human nature."

12. For an impassioned discussion of the power and realism of regional writing, as well as an explication of the connection between the "local" and the "universal" that reinforces a canonical reading of her work, see Eudora Welty, "Place in Fiction," in *The Eye of the Story: Selected Essays and Reviews* (New York: Random House, 1980), pp. 116-33.

13. Lauren Berlant, in "Re-Writing the Medusa: Welty's 'Petrified Man,'" (forthcoming, *Women and Literature*), argues that in the story "the women negate maleness and realign the beauty parlor around female ideology and female sexuality" (16). Berlant's provocative reading suggests that, in context of the story's ironies, Leota and Mrs. Fletcher effectively create a "women's space" where female desires are played out against the submission of Mrs. Pike to a male discourse of competitiveness and the exchange of women. While Berlant's reading attempts a crucial response to the canonized interpretations of Welty's story, our readings disagree sharply over how the story's language can (or may not be able to) *represent* women's discourse.

14. Irigaray, "The Power of Discourse," p. 76. Cixous, "The Laugh of the Medusa," p. 888. See also Nancy K. Miller, "Emphasis Added: Plots and Plausibilities in Women's Fiction," PMLA 96 (1981): 36-48, for an application of Irigaray's ideas about how the philosophic logos can be disrupted by "women's style."

15. Seemingly, my reading to this point appears quite similar to Vande Kieft's, who notices much of the same imagery and declares that "Through a variety of physical, psychological, and cultural irregularities or perversities, the roles of male and female are ironically reversed" (*Eudora Welty*, p. 73). The crucial difference between our readings, however, is that I am insisting the "roles" are not reversed, but repeated, reduplicated. Vande Kieft's reading assumes that there are proper sexual roles which are made improper or parodic through their reversal here. I am arguing, to the contrary, that the story presents a symbolic construction of "male" activities and fantasies which are "proper" to no sex, but which seduce members of both into roles which *reflect* that construction as the incorporation of "male" power.

16. *The Jerusalem Bible* notes of Matthew 16:18 that "Neither the Greek word *petros* nor even, it seems, its Aramaic equivalent *kepha* ('rock') was used as a person's name before Jesus conferred it on the apostles' leader to symbolize the part he was to play in the foundation of the Church. This change of name had possibly been made earlier, cf. Jn. 1:42; Mk 3:16; Lk 6:14" (note f). This would seem to confirm the idea that Jesus' naming of Peter is punningly symbolic, as was the later entitlement of him as *pater*, *papa*, or pope.

17. Irigaray, "The Power of Discourse," p. 79.

18. For a semiotic discussion of the powerful image of the mother in Western art, see Julia Kristeva, "Motherhood According to Giovanni Bellini," in *Desire in Language: A Semiotic Approach to Literature and Art*,

trans. Leon Roudiez et al. (New York: Columbia University Press, 1980), pp. 237-70.

19. In "The Laugh of the Medusa," Cixous suggests that the power of the Medusa lies in its refusing configuration within a mirrored male discourse—a concept "Petrified Man" articulates implicitly, as I shall show momentarily, in its interstices, or in what escapes the mirrored images of the women it represents.

20. Bakhtin, *The Dialogic Imagination*, p. 11.

21. Ibid., p. 7.

22. Cixous, "The Laugh of the Medusa," p. 888.

23. Irigaray, "The Power of Discourse," pp. 73, 75.

24. Berlant's reading of Billy Boy's final comment highlights the contrast between our approaches. While I view this comment as opening up the discourse of the story, Berlant argues that "Because the ideology of wealth and intelligence is alien to the ideal discursive economy of the beauty parlor, the question he asks petrifies the story—the story ends. Billy Boy's gesture does *to* the text what acts of violence do to women *in* the text, and in the mythology which accompanies it" (15-16). This again is to suggest that there is some representation of women's discourse in the story itself with which Billy Boy's male discourse does battle, whereas I question the possibility of representing women's discourse, or the plausibility of these women having escaped the rule of representation.

3. New Visions, New Methods: The Mainstreaming Experience in Retrospect

Without quite knowing what awaited me, I agreed to participate in the NEH-sponsored curriculum integration project at the University of Arizona during the summer of 1982. I had been generally aware of the women's movement, and, having had a graduate student interested in contemporary women's literature in India, I had been casually reading in feminist literary criticism. However, I had not, up to that time, been seriously involved with women's materials in either my research or teaching. In fact, when the formal part of the project began in late May, I had just returned from India, where I had spent four months conducting research on a well-known Urdu writer and filmmaker. I was anxious to work on the materials I had brought back about him and other Urdu writers in the Bombay film industry. On the other hand, I wanted to be able to guide my graduate student in women's literature more effectively, and I was genuinely curious about the discoveries made by "the new scholarship on women," as Catharine Stimpson had phrased it in a kick-off address for the project. With mixed feelings, therefore, I put aside my Urdu materials and plunged into the work of the project.

We began with an all-day opening workshop, in which Women's Studies faculty members associated with the project introduced some of the broader issues generated by recent scholarship on women. Of the readings we had been asked to prepare in advance of that session, Michelle Rosaldo's "Woman, Culture and Society: A Theoretical Overview"[1] provided a good general survey of recent anthropological literature on women and provoked my thinking about various aspects of women's social roles. On the other hand, Annette Kolodny's "Dancing Through the Minefield: Some Observations on the Theory, Practice and Politics of a Feminist Literary Criticism,"[2] which I had been asked to read because of my previous teaching and research on South Asian literature, raised issues not then being discussed by South Asianists, leaving me feeling bewildered and confused. At the session itself, while many of my male colleagues took issue with the various presentations, I often found myself nodding in agreement, especially during a historian's presentation of nineteenth-century medical views of women and a management instructor's discussion of women in management. The final presentation, a slide show of wonderful works by women artists from antiquity to the present, none of whom is mentioned in Jansson's standard history of Western art, left me shaking my head and eager to embark on my own attempt to redress that imbalance.

After the initial session, participants met together both in a larger interdisciplinary group and also in smaller groups broken up according to discipline. Following the suggestions of a faculty member from the English Department, I spent several weeks reading in the areas of feminist literary criticism and women in South Asia and the Middle East. Using suggestions of other project leaders and participants, and ideas generated by the summer's reading, I attempted to make at least a few small changes in two of the courses I was scheduled to teach in the fall of 1982.

Since that first summer, I have continued to be involved with project people and activities and with the Women's Studies program in general. I have attended most of the sessions of our ongoing feminist theory group, as well as the presentations of numerous guest lecturers. Because of changes in the directions of both my research and my teaching, I have developed an extensive bibliographical file not only on South Asian and Middle Eastern women but also on women's history, women and religion, and women and literature. I have been reading widely in areas germane to both my research and coursework, and, insofar as possible, I have tried to include this material in my teaching. By way of furthering my exposure to Women's Studies faculty and materials, I obtained my department's support to attend the National Summer Institute in Women's Studies at the University of Michigan in July 1983.

As I look back over the last two years, I can see quite clearly that involvement in the project has brought about significant changes in both my professional and my personal life. Although I am still sorting them out, these changes seem most visible in three main areas: my teaching strategies, the direction of my research, and my personal intellectual orientation. I could not have predicted it in May 1982, but, in these areas at least, I am no longer the person I was three years ago.

Teaching Strategies and Approaches

Before I participated in the mainstreaming project my teaching responsibilities involved relatively standard courses of the South Asia section of the Oriental Studies department. These courses included the first semester of Oriental Humanities, a large introductory survey course covering, in the fall, the religion, literature, and art of South Asia and the Middle East; Indian Literature in Translation, a two-semester survey course covering classical Sanskrit literature in the fall and contemporary regional literature in the spring; and several levels of Hindi-Urdu language and literature.

The changes that have taken place in my teaching strategies and approaches seem to have followed a progression from most obvious and easiest to effect to more far-reaching and difficult to put into place. This progression began with *making additions of materials dealing with women into existing courses*. At the very beginning this involved simply expanding basic lecture topics to include mention of women. For example, I began alluding to the roles of women in Sufi communities in a discussion of Islamic mysticism and elaborating on changes in the status of women in South Asia and the Middle East as part of a general discussion of modern social developments. As I gained more familiarity with women's materials, I began to include altogether new lecture topics focusing almost exclusively on women. In the Oriental Humanities class, for example, I developed new lectures on Mirabai and Rabi'a al-'Adawiyya, both famous women mystics. Similarly, in the spring semester of the Literature in Translation course, I developed a lecture on British colonial writers, a significant proportion of whom were women whose writings, with their focus on women's issues, provide a telling counterpoint to the writings of their Indian contemporaries. Adding new lecture topics to existing courses eventually required the use of new texts. I added

Elizabeth Warnock Fernea and Basima Qattan Bezirgan's *Middle Eastern Muslim Women Speak*[3] to the Oriental Humanities class first as an optional then as a required text. I also added many xeroxed handouts to both the Oriental Humanities and literature courses.

The inclusion of new lecture topics and new texts has inevitably led to a need to restructure these courses. In Oriental Humanities especially, new materials would not fit neatly into preexisting categories, and the need for a reordering of lecture topics, with material pulled together in new ways, quickly became apparent to me. This was particularly true with the approach to contemporary literature which I had previously structured according to geographical area. I now put this material together according to common themes across geographical area. The inclusion in the discussion of contemporary literature of women writers whose works are scattered in a wide variety of sources has necessitated the use of a xerox packet for student purchase rather than published texts.

Student reaction to these additions to existing courses has varied. In the Oriental Humanities course, especially, most know nothing of the cultures covered by the course and accept all material unquestioningly. Some have noticed that the course includes more materials on women than they are used to in similar courses, and that I am very interested in women's issues. Of these students, women students have reacted very positively to these materials, while only a few men have reacted negatively.

My next step along the progression of change was the *devising of new courses within departmental lines*. Initially this was prompted by the discovery of new materials on women that did not fit into existing courses at all. At the same time, I felt the desire to expand some subject matter touched on only briefly in other courses. As no one else teaching either South Asia or Middle East courses was dealing significantly with women, the need to develop new courses soon became a real imperative. Reaction among my departmental colleagues to these proposed new courses has generally been positive. The current department head participated himself in the mainstreaming project during the summer of 1983 and consequently enthusiastically supports these kinds of innovations. At least three other Oriental Studies faculty members have also participated in various mainstreaming projects, such that we, together with another woman faculty member whose interest in women's history antedates the mainstreaming project, now form a support group for each other, encouraging each other's interests in women's issues.

The first new course I developed was one on Women in South Asian and Middle Eastern literature, first taught in the spring of 1984. Really several courses in one, which might eventually be separated, the course covers two geographical areas with very different cultural patterns. At the same time, it also includes two approaches to women and literature that are frequently separated. The first half of the course covers images of women in classical literature and includes discussions of Hindu scripture, mythology and mystical literature, and of pre-Islamic poetry, the Qur'an and Islamic mystical literature. These discussions are supplemented by revisionist writings on these subjects by contemporary South Asian and Middle Eastern feminists. The second half of the course covers challanges to traditional images by contemporary South Asian and Middle Eastern women writers. Although men were among the earliest champions of women's emancipation in both these areas, and works by male writers could have been included here, I chose instead to focus exclusively on women's writings in the second part of the course. This focus allowed me to introduce the works of many less well-known women writers and to explore the unique insights and concerns of women about their own situation. I dealt with these writings thematically across both areas, revealing both the similarities of concern and the unique cultural constraints upon these writers. Where appropriate, discussions in the course were supplemented by the writings of such contemporary feminists as Nawal al-Saadawi and Fatimah Mernissi and by audiovisual materials, including Elizabeth Fernea's several thought-provoking films and slides of women in various working situations in India. On the whole, the course was a real learning experience for me, allowing me to expand my expertise in the Middle East (South Asia being my original area) and to discover new writers in both geographical areas.

In 1984-85, because we had a visiting faculty member interested in women and religion, I did not develop any new courses. Instead I helped him develop, and then myself participated in, a seminar on Women Saints in India during the spring of 1985. Beginning with a consideration of women's roles in Hindu theology and in the Indian extended family structure, this course went on, via student presentations, to consider individual saintly female figures. While I gained a great deal of insight into the role of women in the Hindu tradition, insight that will illuminate my future teaching, I also had the unexpected pleasure of serving both as a bibliographic resource for the course and a provoker of substantial discussion.

Two more experimental courses are now in the paperwork channels for 1985-86. The first of these, Missionaries in South Asia, picks up my current research interests and gives substantial attention to the roles of women in the mission enterprise. The second new course, Women in South Asia, parallels an already existing course in our department, Women in East Asia. Beginning with a consideration of the roles of women in ancient India, as alluded to in literary, religious, and historical texts, the course will proceed to examine the changes in women's traditional roles that have been brought about by industrialization, increased education, and contact with Western culture. Further down the road, I hope to develop, with the instructor of the East Asia course, a jointly-taught course on Asian women.

The final step in this progression—so far at least—has been the desire to *develop new courses that cut across departmental lines.* Participation in the mainstreaming project has acquainted me with many colleagues working with women's materials and allied with the Women's Studies program. At the same time, the success, in terms of both student support and intellectually stimulating content, of another crossdepartmental course in which I recently participated, Non-Western Literary Theories, has demonstrated to me that courses cutting across geographical and departmental lines can really work. One such possible course would treat Women Saints across cultures. Parallels with Western saintly figures emerged sufficiently frequently in the Women Saints in India course to convince me that this would be a fruitful and stimulating area for exploration. Another possibility is a course on World Women Writers. Exploring common literary concerns across four or five different cultures, the course could include instructors from Oriental Studies, English, and European language departments, varying in content from year to year according to faculty participation. A final possibility would be a jointly-taught seminar on American women's roles in the mission enterprise, both in the various domestic organizations supporting missionaries and in their various capacities overseas.

Having detailed the changes in my teaching approaches that *have* taken place, it seems only fair to mention one that did not take place. At the 1983 National Summer Institute in Women's Studies a good deal of discussion was given over to what was called feminist pedagogy. This discussion was based on readings from Paulo Freire's *The Pedagogy of the Oppressed* and *Education for Critical Consciousness* and on a few accounts of women's experiences in various teaching situations. Although it was suggested that feminists ought somehow to teach in a less authoritarian manner than most men do, even after three weeks, a clear conception of what feminist pedagogy involves did not emerge. Consequently, I have yet to grasp the real issues here, at least insofar as they relate to teaching style. More importantly, I am aware that many students perceive female professors as less competent than male professors, even when both present the same material. For this reason, I have been very concerned, in my large classes at least, with maintaining an authoritative presence in the classroom. Even my dress, usually a dark suit, and my manner reflect this concern. My smaller classes have always been more informal and have allowed for greater discussion and give-and-take among students. Thus, despite exposure to feminist concerns, deep sympathy with the feminist cause, and significant changes in the content of my courses, my participation in the mainstreaming project and subsequent exposure to women's materials has not resulted in any substantial change, for better or for worse, in my teaching style.

Research Directions

Until 1982 my research had focused on contemporary Urdu fiction. Since most accounts of the history of Urdu literature treat women writers as an afterthought, even though women have been writing in Urdu for well over a hundred years, most of my work focused on the well-known male writers. My Ph.D. dissertation was a critical study of the work of Saadat Hasan Manto (1912-1955), a writer associated with the pre-independence Progressive Writers Movement and notorious for his portrayal of lower-class prostitutes in Bombay. I also did some work on contemporary women writers, especially Qurratulain Hyder and two younger Pakistani authors.

In 1982 I began research on Rajindar Singh Bedi (1915-1985). A contemporary of Manto's and a well-respected Urdu short story writer, Bedi also had a fruitful career in the Bombay film industry, working as a dialogue and screenplay writer and producing and directing his own films. Motivated by a desire to do a comparison of Bedi's short stories and films, I spent the first four months of 1982 collecting data on him and his films and interviewing other Urdu writers working in the Bombay film industry.

In some respects, therefore, the summer of 1982 was the worst possible time for me to participate in the mainstreaming project. Fresh from India, I immediately plunged into unrelated materials in the project, with no opportunity to digest the data I had brought back. Unfortunately, by the end of the summer, I was profoundly dissatisfied with my original research topic, and with male writers in general, and I was eager to turn to some project involving women. Although I managed to present one paper at a major professional conference and crank out a substantial article on Bedi, I will probably not do any more with this material in the near future.

I spent most of 1983 casting around for a new area of research that would allow me to combine my newly found interest in women's materials and my expertise in South Asian history and culture generally and in Urdu literature in particular. I found myself profoundly disturbed by the scant attention critics, writing in either English or Urdu, have paid to women writers in Urdu. Hence I initially thought of doing an extended study of nineteenth-century Urdu women writers, as a way of both rewriting the Urdu literary canon and exploring the roots of the twentieth-century resurgence of the women's movement in India.

By early 1984, however, I found that my thoughts were beginning to run in different directions. I was discouraged by the small amount of material actually available on women writers in Urdu, and I had lost interest in the kinds of questions that are usually the focus of purely literary study. At the same time, I wanted to bring to bear on my research my interest involving women and religion that had also been developing since my participation in the mainstreaming project. Consequently, after much soul-searching and discussion with my department head and colleagues both here and elsewhere, I decided to resurrect my previous interest in modern South Asian history and embark on a long-term research project on American missionary women in South Asia and the characteristic patterns of interaction between them and Indian women during the period of approximately 1870-1930. Since May 1984, I have been reading extensively in the areas of women's history, Indian Church history, women missionaries, and denominational mission histories.

By way of beginning the primary research, I spent four days during spring break 1985 working with Indian mission records in the Presbyterian Historical Society in Philadelphia. I wrote successful proposals for a summer research stipend and travel funds from the University of Arizona that will support full-time attention to this project during the summer and three weeks' further research at the Presbyterian Historical Society. Needless to say, I am very much excited by this project, I find my work on it extremely stimulating, and I feel more enthusiasm for my research now than I have felt in a very long time.

The extensive reading in women's history that took place during the ground-laying phase of this project has also, finally, provided me with the theoretical, or disciplinary, foundation for my interest in women's issues that I did not receive from my initial participation in the mainstreaming project. As I now see it, the central insight of almost all the writing on gender, from historical, anthropological, political, literary and other perspectives, is that gender is a social construct, not something "natural" or God-given, but constructed, patterned, by every society for its own purposes and according to its own ideology. Although to those long immersed in feminist theory such an assertion now seems almost a truism, much nineteenth-century American social and religious rhetoric, indeed much contemporary religious polemic, both Christian and non-Christian, is founded on the assumption of inherent natural differences between the sexes. Moreover, Sherry Ortner, in her provocative article, "Is Female to Male as Nature is to Culture?"[4], has shown that male domination is a nearly universal feature of societies. However, the great varieties of male and female roles, with respect to economics, child-rearing, religious duties, political participation, and other aspects of social life, and, more importantly, the changes that have taken place in various societies over time in response to different social forces, all suggest that gender roles are not only extremely elastic, but, indeed, are only very tenuously, if at all, connected to biology. Rather, gender roles are socially determined for specific purposes.

With this new insight in mind, however, when we look at women in history (or literature or any contemporary religious or social group), we experience a central tension in our attempt to study women, a nearly irreconcilable double vision. On the one hand, the social construction of gender renders women a unique group to be studied separately from men. Because of almost universal gender dimorphism and male dominance, women can be seen, as Joan Kelly (Gadol) observed, as an "inferior caste, a minority group,"[5] an almost universally oppressed group, who, like other racial and ethnic minorities have been historically and socially invisible. For Kelly then, as for others, gender becomes a fundamental category of social analysis, like race, class, or nationality.

On the other hand, the great wealth of contemporary scholarship on women makes abundantly clear that femaleness is not a monolithic category, ensuring that all women, in all times, have had nearly identical experiences. Rather, as Sheila Johansson[6] reminds us, women are separated from each other by race, class, ethnic group, religion, nationality, and culture, so that they appear to share more of a common identity with men of their own immediate group than with women outside that group. Because women therefore experience the restrictions of society and constructions of genders differently, women's status patterns are complex, and their lives must be analyzed along several lines. Although I did not then have the theoretical framework into which to fit my experiences, as an American in South Asia, interacting with a variety of women, I sensed this intuitively, as I observed the differences not only between Indian women and me but also between various groups of Indian women with each other. Very early in the mainstreaming process, the importance of cultural differences among women was also demonstrated to me by Linda Nochlin's controversial article, "Why Have There Been No Great Women Artists?"[7] Searching for something identifiably feminine in women's art, Nochlin instead discovered that in every period of Western art, women's art shared the values, perceptions and techniques of the male artists of that period. After illustrating that discovery with the work of some key figures in the history of women's art, Nochlin then goes on to describe some of the social constraints affecting women's participation in the process of artistic production.

Contemporary scholarship on women also cautions us against seeing women simply as passive victims of patriarchal oppression. Rather, as Gail Minault, a historian of South Asian Muslim women, suggests, we need to see women as social agents, as actively involved in social processes of all kinds.[8] Going one step further, the South Asian sociologist Hanna Papanek, in a review of recent social science research on South Asia, suggests that we as scholars must relinquish the "purdah of scholarship" and connect women to other aspects of social change. Bemoaning the fact that "ideas about women are to be confined to an intellectual zenana, a women's quarter that no man and only selected women should even wish to enter" (p. 129), Papanek suggests that changes in gender roles are one of the major dividing lines for assessing social change, and she urges scholars, both women and men, to place gender at the center of their analysis.[9]

Elisabeth Schussler Fiorenza, in the opening chapters of *In Memory of Her*,[10] herself synthesizing much recent scholarship on women, suggests a way of reconciling our double vision as scholars of women. Suggesting that we locate women simultaneously at both the center and the edge of social relations, she seeks "a theoretical framework that can maintain the dialectical tension of women's historical existence as active participants in history as well as objects of patriarchal oppression" (pp. 85-6). In addition to reconceptualizing history and culture as the product of the experiences of both women and men, Fiorenza sees women's experience of solidarity and unity as a social group (despite real class, race and ethnic differences) as based on "their common historical experience as an oppressed group struggling to become full historical subjects" (p. 86). Because the subject of *In Memory of Her* is a reconstruction of the history of women in the early Church, after considering Michelle Rosaldo's public-private dichotomy and Elise Boulding's concepts of the overlife and underlife of society, Fiorenza hypothesizes that religion has often functioned for women as a "middle zone," between public and private, wherein cults, sects and (more recently) voluntary organizations were often subversive of the patriarchal household and state and thus often served emancipatory functions for women (p. 90).

Fiorenza's synthesis and positing of religion as a "middle ground" provide a stimulating example of the second of the two approaches Jane Lewis suggests are open to us as scholars of women. The first is to continue to study women, past and present, according to established methodologies. The second approach, alluded to also by Papanek and Kelly, is to reexamine history (and literature and society) from a "woman-centered point of view," asking new questions of new topics with new theoretical approaches (p. 57).[11] The theoretical ground I have gained from my reading in women's history has helped me both to understand the validity of my research on American women missionaries in South Asia and to focus it in theoretically interesting ways. Because so little has been written by contemporary historians on the behavior of women missionaries overseas, my study will, if nothing else, serve to make "the invisible woman visible," to use Ann Firor Scott's phrase.[12] More importantly, I hope to be able to show that although women missionaries were marginalized by their own denominational structures, because of the prevailing view of women's influence which both sent them out and determined the emphases of their work among Indian women, they and the women with whom they worked were at the center of some of the most profound changes in Indian society during the last century. Finally, I would like to apply Fiorenza's conception of religion as a middle ground to the experience of women in the mission enterprise, showing that both denominational women's foreign mission boards and women's overseas institutions played emancipatory roles for both American and South Asian women.

By the same token, this groundwork is also helping me to rethink the contents and structures of my courses. In both the more general Oriental Humanities course and the more specific Women in South Asia and Missionaries in South Asia courses, I want to make old texts show us both the marginalization of women in traditional culture and their struggle to break free of restrictive roles. At the same time, I want to reclaim women's history and show, most especially through study of women's own writings and accomplishments, the richness and power of their lives, despite male dominance.

Intellectual and Personal Life

The changes that participation in the mainstreaming project has brought about in my general intellectual and personal life are more diffuse and harder to characterize than the changes visible in my teaching strategies and research interests. Yet they undeniably exist. After three years' involvement with women's materials, I feel very differently about myself, not only in terms of my professional context, but in terms of my personal, religious, and community contexts.

To begin with, participation in the project stimulated in me a continued desire to expand intellectually in the area of women's studies. In the spring of 1983, in preparation for teaching my course in Women in South Asian and Middle Eastern literature, which was then already in the planning stage, I audited the Women in Literature course taught by a woman faculty member of the English department. I attended the National Summer Institute in Women's Studies partly for the same reason. Although most of the materials discussed there were not directly germane to my interests, participation in the institute allowed me further exposure to feminist scholarship, much of which had important parallels with issues in my own area. I also found the extremely stimulating opportunity to explore issues with other women academics from various parts of the country, all of whom were at least partly involved with women's studies programs.

My reading outside of course preparation has also been affected by the project. I subscribe to *Signs* and *Ms.*, and I have been reading extensively not only on women in South Asia and the Middle East, but also, as time permits, on other aspects of women's studies. Even my leisure reading has undergone a change. Some feminists speak of a "click" experience, in which one suddenly understands one's situation as a woman in a new way. Shortly after starting the project, I had such a click experience when I stopped in the middle of Saul Bellow's *The Dean's December*, knowing not only that I would never finish it but also that I would not read another male novelist, of whom I had already read far too many, for a long time. Since then I have been reading with immense pleasure, and also with the shock of recognition, the novels of such writers as Margaret Drabble, Margaret Atwood, Sigrid Undset (all three volumes of *Kristin Lavransdatter* in one go), Alice Walker, Agnes Smedley, Marge Piercy, Doris Lessing, Lisa Alther and many others.

A far more acute shift in intellectual orientation, one might even say a crisis, has occurred in my religious orientation as a result of participation in the project. As an adult convert to the Episcopal Church, I have been actively involved in Church life for the last seventeen years, not only at the local parish level, but, since 1980, at the diocesan level as well. Needless to say, my commitment to the Church has been very serious and important to me. However, involvement with women's materials and the reading I have done since 1982 have sensitized me to many aspects of the history and theology of the Church and the subjugation of women in it. The result has been that I have had to rethink my entire relationship to the Church and refound my commitment to it on a different, more feminist, basis. In the process, I have discovered a great deal about women's contributions to the Church of which I was totally ignorant. Along the way, I have done a great deal of reading in the area of women and religion and have been forced to reconsider many issues in a new light. Books which have aided this process include Rosemary Radford Ruether's *Sexism and God-Talk* and Patricia Wilson-Kastner's *Faith, Feminism and the Christ* among theological studies, Patricia Wilson-Kastner's *A Lost Tradition* and Joanne Haggerud's *The Word for Us* for Church history and biblical translation, Mary Giles' *The Feminine Mystic*, Sara Maitland's *A Map of a New Country* for women in the contemporary Church and Rosemary Radford Reuther's *Disputed Questions* for a personal account of exploration of several contemporary issues, including feminism.[13]

Although my discovery of the feminist critique of traditional religion has razed most of my previous faith structure, I remain committed to the Church, not only out of habit and long commitment, but also because a significant number of feminist historians and theologians are helping me refound that commitment in terms more compatible with my new insights. I subscribe to *Ruach*, the journal of the Episcopal Women's Caucus and to the *Journal of Feminist Studies in Religion*. In addition to finding more significant spiritual friendship with other women I respect in the Church, I am now exploring some of these issues with sympathetic men. On our agenda for the very near future is the formation of a discussion-study group on women in the Church.

With a new level of awareness of issues affecting women in the Church, I am also committed to supporting and effecting change in women's roles, women's self-perceptions, liturgical options, use of religious language and lay theological understandings. Interestingly enough, that the change in my religious interests has become discernible to others was recently brought home to me by another click experience: when a colleague, who I had not realized knew anything of my scholarly interests, recently offered me a book on feminist hermeneutics of the Bible.

To this point, it appears that most of the personal change brought about by involvement with the mainstreaming project has taken place inside my head. In fact, comparatively fewer discernible changes have occurred in my domestic and personal life. Although my husband and I have three children, both of us have always shared equally in child care and the running of our household. Consequently, there has been almost no change here. What change I do see is largely attitudinal. I feel more open to my husband and more positively accepting of my marriage. I also feel a greater sense of personal self-confidence, and more willingness to take risks. Finally, I feel more deeply committed to my profession than I had before, partly because I am truly captivated by my research and teaching and partly because I feel a real desire to serve as a role model for younger women and to make the climate of academe more hospitable to them.

Reflections on my Experiences

This narrative of my experiences following involvement in the mainstreaming project raises a real question for me. When I compare my experiences with those of my male colleagues in the project, even with those of the "successes" who have become significantly involved with women's issues in their teaching and research, it is clear that their reactions to the project have been much more theoretical and abstract than mine, and that few have experienced the depth of personal encounter that I have. Moreover, judging from allusions made by other women scholars at the National Summer Institute of Women's Studies and by other women in the mainstreaming project, my experiences are not unique: other women have reacted similarly to the discovery of the women's movement and feminist scholarship. The question for me then is why? Why did the project strike such a responsive chord, and why particularly at this time? I believe that there are several dimensions to the answer to this question. I also believe that these dimensions are also operative in the lives of other women my age and that they will recognize themselves in my narrative.

In trying to answer the question of why now, I turned toward Lillian Rubin's study *Women of a Certain Age.*[14] I wondered if my reactions to the mainstreaming project reflected part of a midlife search for self. I discovered, however, that I do not really fit Rubin's categories. The women in her study range in age from 35 to 54, with 46 as the average age. In addition, all of them "gave up whatever jobs or careers they may have had in their youth to devote themselves to full-time mothering and housewifery for some significant number of years—usually *at least* ten—after their first child was born (p. 12)." In contrast to these women, I am only 41. More importantly, all of my children were born in the summer, and I *never* gave up my academic career.

Nevertheless, Rubin's study had some valid insights for me that have shed light on my own process. In particular Rubin points to the lack of social support for women's career aspirations. She characterizes the midlife woman's attempt to establish herself in a job or career as particularly difficult,

> . . .partly because her struggle for independence, her pursuit of an internally grounded personal identity, goes on without much social support, indeed until very recently, against all social expectations. That means that, despite a decade of feminist challange, she still suffers guilt and discomfort when moving toward a life of her own. . . (p. 127).

Certainly many women academics, especially married women, have felt much the same thing, sensing that their very presence in the academy is "against all social expectations."

My own experiences mirror Rubin's characterization. I have *always* felt that I was on the cutting edge of social change, in my choice of a college 1,000 miles from home, in my decision to teach English in India after graduation from college and then to go to graduate school, and, most especially in my decision to continue working, despite having children. That this last was particularly against all social expectation became vividly clear to me in another click experience when, seeing me in maternity clothes for the first time, the then head of my department astonished me by asking whether I was planning to leave soon. I will never forget the terrible isolation I felt after the birth of my first child in 1974, when I knew no one who was attempting both to work full time and to care for an infant.

Although our children are well past the infant stage, juggling work and family responsibilities, even with a fully sharing husband and father, has never been easy. We have certainly experienced the lack of sufficient time for oneself, one's spouse, and one's children that all two-career couples endure. In addition, like many women academics I had a difficult and discouraging tenure process which was only resolved in my favor after a second year of review. Although my four months in India in 1982 were extremely productive and stimulating in terms of research, I found the separation from my family emotionally very trying, not to mention the heavy burden on my husband of running the household and caring for the children without me.

Involvement in the mainstreaming project, with the rediscovery it brought of the accomplishments of feminist scholars and the women's movement, validated everything I have done so far. In the afterword to *Women of a Certain Age*, Lillian Rubin stresses the importance in her own life of the influence of the women's movement:

> I find myself thinking about my own life, about the choices I've made, about the years of struggle for my career. I'm grateful—grateful that I live in this age when such options exist; grateful for the presence of a women's movement to support my efforts, to let me know I was not alone (p. 209).

This was my experience too. Feminist scholarship has made me realize that, despite the usual social expectations and the experiences of most of my age-mates, I have a right to be in the academy, that the struggle to bring and keep me here is not only worth it, but right and just, and that I am indeed helping to effect necessary changes in the roles of women in our society. Needless to say, after the trauma of my tenure process and the difficult separation from my family, this realization provided not only a huge ego boost but also a strong motivation for moving forward professionally.

In addition to self-validation, involvement in the project also opened up exciting new intellectual vistas for me. I had not expressly been looking for a new challenge and did not feel bored with my field. In fact, my research in India had just opened up a new area for me, Indian cinema, in which I am still interested. However, involvement with feminist historical, literary, and religious scholarship, much of which has been done by scholars in Western history and literature, has opened up to me vast potential areas for similar research in South Asian history and literature. Although I have not changed careers, but simply added a new dimension to my professional life, there is nonetheless a real feeling of exhilaration in that kind of intellectual stimulation, an exhilaration very much akin to what the women in Rubin's study felt as they began new jobs or careers: "There's exhilaration in that—a joyous, almost wondrous reponse to their own unfolding. And there's a sense of freedom to test and explore self in ways not known before. Powerful experiences, these . . . " (p. 185). No less so when new areas of work open up after ten years in the same field.

Yet, for me at least, these are not intellectual vistas in the abstract that have opened up as a result of the mainstreaming project. Rather, I feel as if involvement with the Women's Studies program, with feminist scholarship and with teaching materials including women, has allowed me to reappropriate my own experience into the academic enterprise. I now have a community of women scholars, both at the University of Arizona and in other professional organizations, with whom to relate, after years of interacting exclusively with men. I can now teach and do research on my half of the human race, after years of relegating women to offhand remarks and brief paragraphs. And although I have been saddened and angered by the discovery that feminine imagery has been largely absent from my religious life, both in scripture and liturgy, I have read enough to be able to hope for the eventual reconciliations of my feminist and religious commitments.

As a result of the mainstreaming experience, I am now aware, in a way that I never was before, that *mine* are the experiences that have been left out of the dominant view of culture. In reappropriating those experiences and investing them with academic visibility, nay respectability, an essential part of me has now joined the academic enterprise. My male mainstreaming colleagues, in contrast, have had to find ways to add new, perhaps ill-fitting, pieces to a version of scholarship which has heretofore fully validated their symbols and experiences. This is ultimately the reason why women react so much more strongly to the mainstreaming process than men. Even if for both of us it requires some dismantling of carefully erected disciplinary structures, for men it is a challenging, perhaps even disintegrating experience, that is perhaps least threateningly dealt with in a theoretical or abstract way. For women, on the other hand, it is an integrating experience, perhaps the first one the academy has allowed us to experience, that eventually affects every part of our lives.

Notes

1. Michelle Zimbalist Rosaldo, "Woman, Culture and Society: A Theoretical Overview," in *Woman, Culture and Society*, Michelle Zimbalist Rosaldo and Louise Lamphere, eds., (Stanford: Stanford University Press, (1974), 17-42.

2. Annette Kolodny, "Dancing Through the Minefield: Some Observations on The Theory, Practice and Politics of a Feminist Literary Criticism," *Feminist Studies* 6, 1 (Spring 1980): 1-25.

3. Elizabeth Warnock Fernea and Basima Qattan Berzirgan, *Middle Eastern Muslim Women Speak* (Austin: University of Texas Press, 1976).

4. Sherry B. Ortner, "Is Female to Male as Nature is to Culture?" in *Woman, Culture and Society*, Rosaldo and Lamphere, eds., (Stanford: Stanford University Press, 1974), pp. 67-87.

5. Joan Kelly-Gadol, "The Social Relation of the Sexes: Methodological Implications of Women's History," *Signs* 1 (Summer 1976): 809-23.

6. Sheila Ryan Johansson, "Herstory as History: A New Field or Another Fad?" in *Liberating Women's History*, ed. Berenice A. Carroll (Urbana: University of Illinois Press, 1976), pp. 400-430.

7. Linda Nochlin, "Why Have There Been No Great Women Artists?" *Art News* 69, 9 (1971): 23-71.

8. Gail Minault, "Women and History: Some Theoretical Considerations," *Samya Shakti* (New Delhi) 1, 1 (July 1983): 59-62.

9. Hanna Papanek, "False Specialization and the Purdah of Scholarship—A Review Article," *Journal of Asian Studies* 44, 1 (November 1984): 127-48.

10. Elisabeth Schussler Fiorenza, *In Memory of Her* (New York: Crossroad, 1984).

11. Jane Lewis, "Women Lost and Found: The Impact of Feminism on History," in *Men's Studies Modified: The Impact of Feminism on the Academic Disciplines*, ed. Dale Spender (New York: Pergamon Press, 1981), pp. 55-72.

12. Ann Firor Scott, *Making the Invisible Woman Visible* (Urbana: University of Illinois Press, 1984).

13. Rosemary Radford Reuther, *Sexism and God-Talk* (Boston: Beacon Press, 1983). Patricia Wilson-Kastner, *Faith, Feminism and the Christ* (Philadelphia: Fortress Press, 1983). Patricia Wilson-Kastner, *A Lost*

Tradition (Washington, D.C.: University Press of America, 1981). Joanne Haggerud, *The Word for Us* (Seattle: Coalition on Women and Religion, 1977). Mary Giles, *The Feminine Mystic* (New York: Crossroad, 1982). Sara Maitland, *A Map of a New Country* (Boston: Routledge and Kegan Paul, 1983). Rosemary Radford Reuther, *Disputed Questions* (Nashville: Abingdon Press, 1982).

14. Lillian Rubin, *Women of a Certain Age* (New York: Harper & Row, 1979).

4. Gender Implications of the Traditional Academic Conception of the Political

When I agreed to participate in the Women's Studies main-streaming project at the University of Arizona, I already saw myself as "enlightened" with respect to feminist issues. Moreover, I felt I had previously developed a feminist perspective on the world and the field—political sociology—in which I work. Accordingly, I expected no major conceptual breakthroughs as a results of my participation. Instead, I was only hoping to gain: (a) systematic exposure to the recent feminist scholarship in my field, that I might incorporate it into my courses; and (b) feedback on ways that I might build gender as a variable into an ongoing study of political activism I was then working on. These more "modest" goals were, indeed, realized. However, so too was the type of conceptual breakthrough I had ruled out. So much for lowered expectations.

The object of this rethinking was the traditional academic conception of the "political" that forms a kind of assumptive backdrop against which research and theorizing in political science and sociology had traditionally occurred. While I had begun to rethink specific theories within these fields in terms of their gender implications and to build gender as a variable into my empirical scholarship, I had left intact the broad conceptual frame within which these theories and studies fit. While critical of the frame on other grounds, I had remained oblivious to its gender implications. Those implications now strike me as rather obvious and indefensible. In the sections that follow, I will attempt to describe the traditional academic conception of the "political," briefly sketch what I see as its important gender implications, and suggest an alternative conceptual frame for studying political phenomena.

The Traditional Academic Conception of the Political

It would seem clear that the category of the "political" — that is, those topics that are properly seen as political — is made up of a wide and diverse range of phenomena. Obviously, the dynamics of formally constituted political parties, institutions, and actors are an important component of the category. But having grown up as part of the generation that came of age during the 1960s, I also find it quite natural to associate the political with noninstitutionalized forms of action—riots, illegal strikes, mass marches—as much as our formal political institutions and processes. Likewise, scholarship on the roots of radical feminism (cf. Evans, 1980) has sensitized us to the power of shared personal experiences to shape collective action. Feminists have also deepened our understanding of the political by making us aware of the fact that questions of power, authority, and control over scarce resources are as germane to those traditionally "private" spheres of life—family, religion, and so on—as to any "public" arenas (Emery, 1982; Thorne and Yalom, 1982; Walker and Thompson, 1984). Finally, still other feminist scholars have contributed to our understanding of the political significance of the intersection of these public and private spheres (Balbo, 1982; Prokop, 1978; Weinbaum and Bridges, 1976).

Yet when we turn our attention to the traditional academic conception of the political, we find none of the richness and diversity embodied in the above topics. Instead, the political is seen as largely synonymous with the realm of institutionalized politics and the behaviors of formally recognized political actors. It is the politics of "proper channels" and "proper authorities." The following list of chapter headings taken from a popular introductory textbook in political science merely serves to underscore this point:

The Irony of Democracy
The Founding Fathers: The Nation's First Elite
The Evolution of American Elites
Men at the Top: Positions of Power in America
Elites and Masses: The Shaky Foundations of Democracy

Elite—Mass Communication: Television, the Press and the
  Pollsters
Elections: Imperfect Instruments of Accountability
American Political Parties: A System of Decay
The Organized Interests: Defenders of the Status Quo
The Presidency
The Bureaucratic Elite and Public Policy
Congress: The Legislative Elite
Courts: Elites in Black Robes
American Federalism: Elites in States and Communities
Protest Movements: Challenge to Dominant Elites
Epilogue: Dilemmas of Politics

(Dye and Zeigler, 1981)

In examining this list one searches in vain for any mention of the
internal politics of family life, the personal roots of radical activism,
the intersection of capital production and family consumption, or
any number of other topics that might imply a broader conception of
the political. Likewise, social movements are only treated in the last
substantive chapter as a kind of special topic, rather than integrated
into the other chapters as a routine component of politics in the
United States. Our attention is thus squarely focused on the formal
political actors (lobbyists, elected officials, civil service bureau-
crats), political institutions (the courts, Congress, the presidency,
political parties), and political processes (elections, court challenges,
lobbying) that comprise our institutionalized system of politics. The
inevitable result of using such a textbook is a class not unlike that of
traditional survey courses in history in which the history of a given
period is seen as synonymous with the public life of the political,
economic, and military elite of society. The message is unmistakable:
politics is something that takes place in public domains between
officially recognized political actors. Moreover, those domains are
defined as masculine—they represent authority, rationality, justice,
and order.

Reflecting the traditional association of the political with public
life, political science has virtually ignored any areas of life seen as
private. These areas may be referenced in passing, for example, in a
discussion on how a particular court case or piece of legislation is
likely to affect them, but the areas themselves remain outside the
universe of political discourse and analysis. Sociology, of course,

does not ignore the more "private" sectors of social life. Courses in the sociology of religion or marriage and the family, to take but two examples, are staples of virtually every college's undergraduate program in sociology. Traditionally, however, the focus in these courses has been decidedly nonpolitical. In classes on marriage and the family, neither the internal politics of family life—centered on such topics as the division of household labor, inequality in power and authority, and gender differences in allocation of resources— nor the larger political/economic functions served by existing family arrangements are granted any real importance. Instead, these crucial issues have been almost totally ignored in favor of a focus on such topics as family roles, mate selection, social and cultural differences in form and size of the family, and socialization within the family. Political topics remain the exclusive province of courses in political sociology or stratification. This division serves to reinforce and reify the traditional distinction between the public and private as well as the political and exclusively "social" spheres of life.

But what of social movements? Surely, a social phenomenon that would include the Russian revolution, the black civil rights movement, women's liberation and the Moral Majority as examples would have to be regarded as fundamentally political in nature. Not so, according to the traditional sociological conception of social movements. Instead, social movements have typically been studied in the context of courses in collective behavior. The latter represents an interesting collection of phenomena, including fads, crazes, cults, and panics, that clearly betrays the apolitical view of social movements that has long held sway in the social sciences. What unites this disparate collection of behaviors is their presumably unstructured or emergent quality. All are seen as collective responses to a social situation that is poorly defined or ambiguous. The ambiguity is experienced as psychologically stressful, thus encouraging collective efforts to reduce or manage the stress. In effect, we are being told that social movements are properly viewed as psychological rather than as political phenomena. The logic is straightforward. As a form of collective behavior, social movements represent an entirely different behavioral dynamic than institutionalized politics. While the latter is generally interpreted as rational action in pursuit of a substantive political goal, social movements have been left, in Gamson's paraphrase of the traditional view, to "the social psychologist whose intellectual tools prepare him to better understand the irrational" (1975:133).

The Gender Implications of the Traditional View

Out of this mix of academic subfields—collective behavior, marriage and the family, political sociology, and so on—one can discern the broad outlines of a traditional academic conception of the political. Because this conception is grounded in unacknowledged and unexamined assumptions about gender, authority, and political life, it operates to reinforce and lend "scientific" legitimacy to a number of traditional views regarding the "nature" of men and women and the suitability of each to various roles in society. In particular, I want to analyze three interrelated problems in the literature and their gender implications.

DISTINCTION BETWEEN THE PUBLIC AND PRIVATE

One effect of this academic division of labor is to reify the familiar distinction between the public and private spheres of life. This occurs through the association of each with its own distinct set of subfields and attendant courses. Within sociology, "private" spheres of life have tended to merit courses of their own. So, for example, an undergraduate at most universities would be able to take courses in the Sociology of Religion, Marriage and the Family, and Social Psychology. The "public" side of life would be represented in such classes as Political Sociology, Complex Organizations, and Social Stratification. In political science, the public/private mix of subfields and classes would not be so balanced. Given the traditional association of the public with the political, one would find most subfields within political science squarely focused on "public life." Courses on Political Parties, the American Presidency, The Judicial Process, and Governmental Bureaucracy would be standard fare in undergraduate political science offerings. By making each sphere synonymous with certain subfields and related courses, academia has gone a long way to depicting the public/private split as "natural" or "normal." But as Rosaldo (1974) and others have argued, there is nothing "natural," that is to say, inevitable, about this split. Rather, it is the product of socially constructed cultural practices and institutions that may well have their roots in the child-bearing and child-rearing activities of women. The fact that this split is far more pronounced in some cultures than others only serves to underscore the social origins and maintenance of the public/private distinction (Rosaldo, 1974: 36-37). Instead of reifying this distinction, then, we should be making it a topic for study in its own right.

THE NONPOLITICAL NATURE OF PRIVATE LIFE

The subfield stucture of political science and sociology does more than simply reinforce the notion of public and private spheres of life. It does so in such a way as to assign political significance to the public while denying it to the private, by virtue of the topics and issues addressed in the various classes that serve to define the public/private split. Classes in political science and political sociology are, of course, explicitly political in their focus. Courses focused on the traditionally "private" sectors of life, however, have tended to be nonpolitical in their emphasis. Consider my earlier example of courses in Marriage and the Family, perhaps the most significant instance of this de-politicizing tendency. While it would seem obvious that the family is rich in political significance both in its internal structure and its relationship to the larger political system, this perception does not ordinarily inform the curriculum of such courses. Instead, topics covered tend to focus on the ostensibly nonpolitical aspects of family life. The table of contents of a popular text for Marriage and the Family courses will serve to illustrate this focus:

Life Designs: Concepts and Approaches

The Acquisition of Gender Identities and Roles

From Childhood to Adolescence: Sources and Contexts of Change

Pathways to Partners: Sociocultural Dimensions of Partner Selection in the Contemporary United States

Living Together Before Marriage

Pregnancy Before Marriage: Contraception, Abortion and Out-of-Marriage Births

The Beginnings of Marriage

The Psychosocial Interior

Marital Sexuality

Fertility and the Family Life Cycle

Men and Women in the Labor Force

The Labor of the Household

The Ties of Kinship and Friendship

Intimate and Erotic Relations Outside Marriage

The Impact of Change and Crisis

Ending Marriages

After Divorce and Death

The Single Alternative

(Gagnon and Greenblatt, 1978: xviii-xxiii)

Certainly these topics are important and deserving of attention. What is less defensible is the almost total absence of any explicitly political content in the list of chapters. In particular the list would seem to suffer from three glaring deficiencies.

1. *The dynamic relationship between the political system and the family.* While our families may seem to be distant and separate from the political system, they nonetheless are locked in a profoundly important dialectical relationship with the state (Boris and Bardaglio, 1983). On the one hand, the structure and function of the family is powerfully affected by a wide range of policies and programs generated and administered by the state. As examples, one could cite tax policies for single and married persons, federal guidelines regulating the provision of aid to dependent children and laws that restrict police intervention in cases of spouse abuse. More important than any single piece of legislation, however, is the more fundamental way in which the state treats men and women as gendered creatures in all of its deliberations (Mackinnon, 1983). It therefore not only influences on family life but does so in ways that serve to reproduce gender relations and the inequities associated with these relations. More subtly, the state acts, through its system of public education, as a powerful agent socializing children into adult roles. Thus, it is largely through state-supported schools that young people are oriented to the occupational roles that so profoundly shape the dynamics of family life in contemporary America.

The family does not, however, stand in an exclusively passive

position with respect to the state. It is not only the fundamental
social unit on which the state is based, it also helps shape the political
context in which the state acts. Two examples will serve to illustrate
the point. Demographic trends are, in one sense, merely the
aggregation of individual family planning decisions. To the extent,
then, that such trends exert enormous pressure on the state to enact
demographically sound fiscal, educational, and economic policies,
the family may be said to be indirectly shaping government action.
More importantly the state and attendant political system is
enormously dependent on the family as the principal agent of
political socialization. It is a well-known and consistently demonstrated fact that the best predictor of children's political attitudes is
parents' political attitudes (cf. Jennings and Niemi, 1968). The same
holds true for party affiliation. Given that the alignment of political
forces and the control of major elective positions are crucially affected by prevailing attitudes and party preferences, one begins to
appreciate the important determinant role played by the family in
shaping the broad contours of political life.

　　2. *The internal politics of family life.* More germane to the topic of
gender and politics is the application of a political perspective to the
internal life of the family. Quite simply, the central political
questions of governance, distribution of power and authority, and
equality/inequality are as relevant to the family as to society as a
whole (cf. Bell and Newby, 1976). The recent public attention to the
phenomena of spouse and child abuse within the family only serves
to underscore this point with contemporary poignancy (cf. Mills,
1985). Although the sociological literature on marital power
acknowledges this reality, it has so far offered little analysis of the
relationship between other political institutions and the internal
politics of family life.

　　When examining family politics it is important not to view
women as the passive victims of an oppressive patriarchy. Far from
it. In spite of severe legal and normative constraints, women have
probably contested more successfully for power and influence
within the family than in any other major sphere of life. As more and
more married women have entered the labor force, they have been
able to use the greater financial resources paid employment has
afforded them to more nearly equalize their decision-making
influence at home. Even in traditional families, however, women's
status as primary caregivers has often given them a kind of monopoly

on the emotional loyalties of children. In turn, these loyalties can and have been used as a powerful weapon in power struggles with husbands. Finally, control over sexual access grants women yet another source of leverage in any contest for power or influence within the family.[3]

The dynamics alluded to here seriously contradict the traditional academic conception of the political. Women in this conception emerge as apolitical. Having restricted their focus to those institutionalized political arenas from which women have traditionally been excluded, women are implicitly depicted as apolitical. This conclusion is reinforced by the nonpolitical focus on family life characteristic of academic treatments of the subject. However, when we view the family politically, women emerge as being as concerned with issues of power, governance, equity and the like as men. Moreover, women's concern with power within the family has also shaped their associational and political activities more generally (Ryan, 1983).

3. *Gender mediation between state and family*. Finally, when combined, the internal politics of family life and the structure of state/family relations yields a third topic deserving of attention. The topic concerns the crucial role played by women, acting in their traditional roles as wives and mothers, in mediating between the family and the political economy. Laura Balbo (1982: 251) has referred to this crucial mediating function as "the servicing work of women." What Balbo and other authors have in mind is a complex set of activities that tend to fall to women because of traditional sex role socialization and the internal power dynamics of family life. These activities can be characterized as "*consumption work* with women as the central mediators between the profit market, state services and the needs of the family" (Balbo, 1982: 252). This involves women not only in a range of fairly routine tasks such as shopping and household maintenance (cf. Weinbaum and Bridges, 1976), but more complex activities centering around the acquisition and provision of various "services".

> Many goods and services are produced outside the family by other institutions (firms, schools, hospitals). Because such resources make up a crucial part of the total available resources and because access to them requires time and flexibility on the part of "clients," someone has to do the work of dealing with these agencies,

adapting to their often complex, time-consuming, rigid, indeed "bureaucratic" procedures. It is women who keep in touch with teachers and school staff, who take children to clinics and hospitals, who visit welfare agencies to obtain what the family is entitled to. (Balbo 1982: 253)

As described by Balbo, this "consumption work" has enormous implications at both the individual and societal leval. At the individual level, it saddles women with a set of responsibilities that men feel only more lightly. It thus acts to limit the time and energy women have to devote to other pursuits, including careers. It also minimizes the pressures on men and on major social institutions to promote changes which would reduce these contradictions and promote gender equality. The end result is the perpetuation of occupational inequalities and the exacerbation of the "superwoman" pressures many women feel in trying to juggle family and career responsibilities.

At the societal level, this pattern of "consumption work" serves to privatize and, thus, to obscure the contradictions inherent in the post-industrial service economy. More to the point, it places the burden of resolving those contradictions squarely in the hands of women. If mother is too infirm to maintain her own residence, but lacks the resources to afford to live in one of the few attractive for-profit nursing homes, then the family faces a choice. Either she can be confined to a drab, lifeless, state-supported facility or maintained at home. Either way, it is likely that the burden of care or visitation will fall to the woman of the house. The same is true in countless other cases where the demands of a profit economy and the limits of state largesse combine to impose exceptional service demands on the family. By stepping into the breach, wives and mothers have traditionally saved the system from its own contradictions (Abel, 1986). The political and economic significance of this solution would be hard to exaggerate.

THE REINFORCEMENT OF THE TRADITIONAL ARISTOTELIAN VIEW OF MEN AND WOMEN

But perhaps the most significant aspect of the academic conception of the political is how well it accords with the traditional Western view of men and women, maleness and femaleness. That view has deep roots in the Western philosophic tradition drawing support from sources as diverse as the Bible, classical Greek philosophy, and medieval theology. The conception is based on the idea that women and men are *inherently* different from one another, characterlogically as well as biologically. Indeed, the biological differences are usually seen as the root cause of the differences in personality or character. However the differences are explained, the basic assumption remains the same: men and women diverge sharply in their "basic natures." And what are these basic natures? While writers in the tradition may disagree on certain minor points, their basic portraits of men and women remain remarkably consistent over time. The broad contours of the traditional conception of women is nicely captured in the following statements by Aristotle and Freud. First Aristotle:

> In all cases, excepting those of the bear and leopard, the female is less spirited than the male . . . . With all other animals the female is softer in disposition than the male, is more mischievous, less simple, more impulsive, and more attentive to the nurture of young; the male, on the other hand, is more savage, more simple and less cunning. The traces of these differentiated characteristics are more or less visible everywhere, but they are especially visible where character is the more developed, and most of all in man. The fact is, the nature of man is the most rounded off and complete, and consequently in man the qualities or capacities above referred to are found in their perfection. Hence woman is more compassionate than man, more easily moved to tears, at the same time is more jealous, more querulous, more apt to scold or strike. She is, furthermore, more prone to despondency and less hopeful than the man, more void of shame or self-respect, more false of speech, more deceptive . . . .   (Osborne, 1979: 37)

And Freud:

> . . . women have but little sense of justice, and this is no doubt connected with the preponderance of envy in their mental life; for the demands of justice are a modification of envy; they lay down the conditions under which one is willing to part with it. We say also of women that their social interests are weaker than those of men, and that their capacity for the sublimation of their instincts is less.   (Freud, 1933: 183)

The image is clear. Women are more emotional, more expressive, and less rational than men. "Their social [read: public] interests
are weaker than those of men." Finally they have less ability to
invoke abstract, objective conceptions of justice than do men. (In
case the reader feels these views are merely the outdated ideological
artifacts of earlier eras, consider that this latter characterization finds
contemporary expression in Kohlberg's influential work—e.g., Kohlberg and Kramer, 1969; Kohlberg, 1971—on stages of moral
development. See Gilligan, 1979, for a critique of Kohlberg.)

Based on this conception of men and women, which group
would you say was better suited to political leadership? Emotional,
expressive women or men with their greater capacity for dispassion-
ate, instrumental action in pursuit of universalistic ends? In short,
this conception also contains the strong suggestion that men, but not
women, are fit for public political life.

So what? What does this view have to do with the traditional
academic conception of the political? The answer, of course, is:
everything. In that conception, institutionalized politics is synonymous with rational political action while social movements are
relegated to the status of expressive, coping mechanisms. Clearly
visible in this distinction are our old friends, Aristotelian man and
Aristotelian woman. By virtue of his dominance and dispropor-
tionate representation within institutionalized political arenas, man
emerges as the embodiment of rational, instrumental politics. In
turn, woman's absence from those arenas merely "confirms" her
nonpolitical "nature." Where she *does* become visible is in her
participation in social movements. But far from contradicting the
characterization of women as apolitical, this involvement merely
confirms it. For remember what the underlying motives for
movement participation are. According to sociologist, William
Kornhauser, "mass movements are not looking for pragmatic
solutions to economic or any other kind of problem. If they were so
oriented, their emotional fervor and chiliastic zeal . . . would not
characterize the psychological tone of these movements. In order to
account for this tone, we must look beyond economic interests to
more deep-seated psychological tendencies" (1959: 163). And what
are these tendencies? Another sociologist, Neil Smelser, offers one
possibility: "The striking feature of the protest movement is what
Freud observed: it permits the expression of impulses that are
normally repressed . . . The efforts—sometimes conscious and

sometimes unconscious—of leaders and adherents of a movement to create issues, to provoke authorities . . . would seem to be in part efforts to 'arrange' reality so as to 'justify' the expression of normally forbidden impulses in a setting which makes them appear less reprehensible to the participants" (1973: 317). Thus woman's participation in movements merely reflects her emotional, expressive "nature" and her reduced capacity for sublimation. Her "essential nature" is confirmed, then, by her lack of participation in rational—read: institutionalized—politics as well as her "affinity" for social movements.

This traditional conception of social movements also has important implications for how we approach the question of agency in instances of political change. The traditional view would seem to deny to social movements any potential for significant social change. The social movement is effective, not as political action, but as therapy. To be sure, movements are not unrelated to politics. Smelser, for example, tells us that they frequently represent a precursor to effective political action (1962: 73). Movements, in this view, function as a kind of early warning system, alerting the political establishment to sources of strain that must be attended to if these "aberrant" forms of behavior are to subside.

Consider the gender implications of this view when applied to any of the three major feminist movements to arise in the United States. If we take this view seriously, credit for the substantive changes that followed from these movements is due, not to feminists, but the male legislators who responded with foresight and rationality to the inchoate and expressive demands of the movement. Women find themselves once more in an all too familiar position; dependent upon men and their greater "natural" endowments for their well being. Liberal male largesse is once again seen as the source of progressive social change.

Alternative Conception of Women and the Political

One can, of course, advance alternative conceptions of both "woman" and the political. As regards woman, it would seem impossible to know what her "essential nature" is apart from socialization. Since we only encounter "her" after socialization is underway, it is as likely that "her" characteristics reflect the effects of nurture rather than nature. Certainly the rich variety of identities and attributes displayed by women cross-culturally lends credence to this view (cf. Rosaldo and Lamphere, 1974). Any fit, then, between women's "nature" and politics is likely to be culturally specific and socially constructed.

This brings us back to the political. The above distinction between rational institutionalized politics and irrational social movements requires that we assume the openness of the political system. For if the system is closed, participation in it can hardly reflect the simple expression of "natural" political abilities. Instead, to the degree that it is closed, participation begins to reflect one's socially determined access to the system. Similarly, in the face of a closed political system, it becomes difficult to attribute social movements to the "deep-seated psychological" needs of its adherents. Rather, as in the contemporary case of South Africa, movements reflect the efforts of disenfranchised groups to achieve substantive political goals outside "proper channels" that have traditionally been closed to them.[4]

Social movements, in this view, are not a form of irrational behavior but rather a tactical response to the harsh realities of a closed and coercive political system. Viewed in this light, the distinction between movement behavior and institutionalized politics disappears. Both should be seen as rational attempts to pursue collective interests. Differences in behavior between movement participants and institutionalized political actors are attributable, not to the cognitive or psychological inadequacies of the former, but to the different strategic problems confronting each.

Therefore, if women have more often used social movements to advance their interests than men, that fact tells us more about each group's access to "proper channels" than it does about any differences in the inherent capacity of men or women to engage in rational political action. Conversely, if we have traditionally found fewer women than men in positions of institutionalized political power, it is only because they have faced greater social and cultural— and sometimes legal—barriers to participation. Indeed, in those political arenas where few or no barriers to participation exist, women's rates of participation tend to be comparable to those of men (cf. Carroll, 1979: Diamond, 1977). In short, no one has yet produced any systematic evidence to show that women are inherently any less (or more) political than men. To the extent that the traditional academic conception of the political suggests as much, it serves to distort not only the nature of institutionalized politics and social movements, but also the role of men and women in each.

Notes

1. I would like to thank Karen Anderson, Pat MacCorquodale and Trudy Mills for their extremely helpful comments on an earlier draft of this paper.

2. One can note an occasional exception to this general rule. One such exception is Randall Collins' (1985) textbook entitled *Sociology of Marriage and the Family: Gender, Love and Property*, in which he analyzes the family as a system of property relationships.

3. Not that this control is absolute. The reality of marital rape and the reluctance of the police to intervene in "domestic quarrels" should be enough to remind us of how deeply ingrained the conception of the wife as the husband's property is in our culture.

4. This conception is very much at the heart of two models of social movements that, within the last fifteen years, have replaced the older tradition as the dominant perspective on social movements within political sociology. These are the resource mobilization (McCarthy and Zald, 1973, 1977) and political process (McAdam, 1982; Tilly, 1978) models of collective action.

References

Abel, Emily K. 1986. "Adult Daughters and Care For the Elderly." *Feminist Studies* 12: 479-497.

Balbo, Laura. 1982. "The Servicing Work of Women and the Capitalist State." in *Political Power and Social Theory*, vol. 3, Maurice Zeitlin (ed.). Greenwich, CT: JAI Press, pp. 251-270.

Bell, Colin, and Howard Newby. 1976. "Husbands and Wives: The Dynamics of the Deferential Dialectic." In *Dependence and Exploitation in Work and Marriage*. Diana Barker and Sheila Allen (eds.). New York: Longman.

Boris, Eileen, and Peter Bardaglio. 1983. "The Transformation of Patriarchy: The Historic Role of the State." In *Families, Politics, and Public Policy: A Feminist Dialogue on Women and the State*. Irene Diamond (ed.). New York: Longman.

Carroll, Berenice, A. 1979. "Political Science, Part I: American Politics and Political Behavior." *Signs* (no. 2): 289-306.

Chodorow, Nancy. 1980. "Gender, Relation, and Difference in Psychoanalytic Perspective." In *The Future of Differences*. Hester Eisenstein and Alice Jardine (eds.). Boston: G.K. Hall, pp. 3-19.

Chodorow, Nancy. 1974. "Family Structure and Feminine Personality." In *Woman, Culture, and Society*. Michelle Rosaldo and Louise Lamphere (eds.). Stanford: Stanford University Press, pp. 43-66.

Collins, Randall. 1985. *Sociology of Marriage and the Family: Gender, Love and Property*. Chicago: Nelson-Hall.

Diamond, Irene. 1977. *Sex Roles in the State House*. New Haven, CT: Yale University Press.

Dye, Thomas R., and L. Harmon Zeigler. 1981. *The Irony of Democracy*. Monterey, CA: Duxbury Press.

Emery, Mary. 1982. "The Contemporary Family: Reproduction, Production, Consumption." *Free Inquiry in Sociology* 10: 95-104.

Evans, Sarah. 1980. *Personal Politics*. New York: Vintage Books.

Freud, Sigmund. 1933. *New Introductory Lectures on Psycho-Analysis*. New York: W.W. Norton & Company, Inc.

Gagnon, John, and Cathy S. Greenblatt. 1978. *Life Designs*. Glenview, IL: Scott, Foresman and Company.

Gamson, William A. 1975. *The Strategy of Social Protest*. Homewood, IL: Dorsey Press.

Gilligan, Carol. 1979. "Women's Place in Man's Life Cycle." *Harvard Educational Review* 49 (no. 4): 431-46.

Horney, Karen. 1939. *New Ways in Psychoanalysis*. New York: W.W. Norton & Company, Inc.

Jennings, M.K., and R.G. Niemi. 1968. "The Transmission of Political Values from Parent to Child." *American Political Science Review* 62: 169-84.

Kohlberg, L., and R. Kramer. 1969. "Continuities and Discontinuities in Childhood and Adult Moral Development." *Human Development* 12: 93-120.

Kohlberg, L. 1971. "From is to Ought: How to Commit the Naturalistic Fallacy and Get Away With it in the Study of Moral Development." In *Cognitive Development and Epistemology*. T. Mischel (ed.). New York: Academic Press, pp. 151-235.

Kornhauser, William. 1959. *The Politics of Mass Society*. Glencoe, IL: The Free Press.

MacCormack, Carol P. 1980. "Nature, Culture and Gender: A Critique." In *Nature, Culture and Gender*. Carol P. MacCormack and Marilyn Starthern (eds.). London: Cambridge University Press, pp. 1-24.

MacKinnon, Catharine A. 1983. "Feminism, Marxism, Method, and the State: Toward Feminist Jurisprudence." *Signs: Journal of Women in Culture and Society* 8: 635-658.

McAdam, Doug. 1982. *Political Process and the Development of Black Insurgency, 1930-1970*. Chicago: University of Chicago Press.

McCarthy, John, and Mayer N. Zald. 1977. "Resource Mobilization and Social Movements: A Partial Theory." *American Journal of Sociology* 82: 1212-1241.

———, 1973. *The Trend of Social Movements in America: Professionalism and Resource Mobilization*. Morristown, NJ: General Learning Press.

Mead, Margaret. 1975. "On Freud's View of Female Psychology." In *Women and Analysis: Dialogues on Psychoanalytic Views of Femininity*. Jean Strouse (ed.). New York: Grossman, pp. 95-106.

Mills, Trudy. 1985. "The Assault on the Self: Stages in Coping with Battering Husbands." *Qualitative Sociology* 8:103-123.

Ortner, Sherry. 1974. "Is Female to Male as Nature is to Culture?" In *Woman, Culture, and Society*. Michelle Rosaldo and Louise Lamphere (eds.). Stanford: Stanford University Press, pp. 67-87.

Osborne, Martha Lee (ed.). 1979. *Women in Western Thought*. New York: Random House.

Pateman, Carole. 1980. "The Disorder of Women: Women, Love, and the Sense of Justice." *Ethics* 91: 20-34.

Prokop, Ulrike. 1978. "Production and the Context of Women's Daily Life." *New German Critique* 13: 18-33.

Rosaldo, Michelle Zimbalist. 1974. "Women, Culture and Society: A Theoretical Overview." In *Woman, Culture, and Society*. Michelle Zimbalist Rosaldo and Louise Lamphere (eds.). Stanford, CA: Stanford University Press, pp. 17-43.

Rosaldo, Michelle Zimbalist, and Louise Lamphere (eds.). 1974. *Woman, Culture, and Society*. Stanford, CA: Stanford University Press.

Ryan, Mary. 1983. *Womanhood in America*. New York: Watts.

Shulman, Alix Kates. 1980. "Sex and Power: Sexual Bases of Radical Feminism." *Signs* 5 (no. 4): 590-604.

Smelser, Neil. 1962. *Theory of Collective Behavior*. New York: Free Press of Glencoe.

——, 1973. "Social and Psychological Dimensions of Collective Behavior." In *The Sociology of Revolution*. Ronald Ye-Lin Cheng (ed.). Chicago: Henry Regnery, pp. 314-18.

Thorne, Barrie, and Marilyn Yalom (eds.). 1982. *Rethinking the Family*. New York: Longman.

Tilly, Charles. 1978. *From Mobilization to Revolution*. Reading, MA: Addison-Wesley.

Walker, Alexis, and Linda Thompson. 1984. "Feminism and Family Studies." *Journal of Family Issues* 5: 545-570.

Weinbaum, Batya, and Amy Bridges. 1976. "The Other Side of the Paycheck: Monopoly Capital and the Structure of Consumption." *Monthly Review* 29: 89-103.

GARY F. JENSEN

5. Mainstreaming and the Sociology of Deviance: A Personal Assessment

Introduction

When I was a teenager, I often attended Saturday night dances sponsored by the city recreation department at the Veteran's Hall in my hometown. Most of my time, like that of most of my friends, was spent standing on the sidelines trying to get up nerve to ask a girl to dance. One of those Saturday nights a casual acquaintance was taking on all comers in finger wrestling: interlocking middle fingers and twisting until someone gives. I hoped he would not get to me since I had watched him beat several other people and it looked like it hurt. However, after defeating several other boys he turned and challenged me. As a teenage male in American society I felt I had no real choice but to accept. Even though I had numerous alternative sources of pride (high grades, student leadership, track, etc.) I could not back down. The match ended in a draw although, secretly, I would have declared the opponent the winner since he had cracked my finger without knowing it. At least I had not been humiliated.

While the incident seems trivial in a society perennially plagued by crime and serious violence, it reflects certain common experiences in the adolescent male world. Boys live in a world of pervasive competition, challenge, interpersonal aggression, and violence. To hide from it, to try to talk one's way out of it or to show fear is to risk being called a "wimp," a "pussy" or, even more recently, a "wussy." A mere verbal response would compound the problem and further justify such labels.

77

Teenage males in such situations are likely to feel they have no choice even though they are aware of justifications for other responses. For example, I was aware of the "turn-the-other-cheek" philosophy, but that was an abstract notion which seemed totally irrelevant to the situation. A male who turned the other cheek was vulnerable to an endless line of competitors and to loss of status and respect as well. There were no points for idealism, and losing was more respectable than refusing to play the game.

What do such situations have to do with mainstreaming feminist scholarship at American universities? The major goal of mainstreaming is to incorporate material by and about women into the normal course of higher education. However—whether or not this is among its intents—such mainstreaming may be the only way for males to understand themselves, since it is through the study of women that males can come to understand the constraints shaping their own choices, the basis for their fears, and the prospects for alternative futures. Moreover, since most forms of violence and destruction are more typically male than female, the study of gender and deviance may ultimately help us learn how to keep from destroying ourselves. Any answers will be found in the study of both the male and female worlds and the points of similarity and conflict between them.

The remainder of this paper is devoted to a personal assessment of scholarship by and about women in relation to my own area of expertise—the sociology of deviance. It is organized around several observations prompted by my experience reviewing recent feminist scholarship. First, while the study of gender in relation to deviance has developed into one of the most popular topics in criminological research, the most frequently cited works by women specifically addressing female crime and gender differences in crime have merely applied existing theories which deny any unique value to the female world. Secondly, feminist critics of existing research techniques in the study of deviance (and social issues in general) attribute problems to methodology which would more appropriately be attributed to inadequate, narrow and superficial use of existing tools. In doing so, feminist critics fail to recognize the relevance of their own criticisms to their narrow image of science. Finally, progress in the explanation of gender differences in deviance is likely to emerge through the use of existing research tools to study those general ideas raised by feminist scholars interested in basic issues involving justice, morality and parenting. In contrast to the simplistic approach of criminologists, such scholars perceive both authentic value and costs associated with both the female and male worlds. Each of these observations or claims will be elaborated below.

The "New" Focus on Women in the Sociology of Deviance

For most of the history of criminology it would be accurate to state that women received relatively little attention as compared to men. However, since the mid-1970s the study of women and crime has developed into one of the most popular topics in the field. In 1975 two major monographs appeared: Rita Simon's *Women and Crime* and Freda Adler's *Sisters in Crime*. Carol Smart's *Women, Crime and Criminology*, published in 1976, was followed by numerous other works (Bowker 1978; Adler and Simon 1979; Datesman and Scarpitti 1980; Warren 1981; Weisberg 1982; Schur 1984). A growing body of empirical research can be found in professional journals as well (e.g., see Weiss 1976; Jensen and Eve 1976; Harris 1977; Cernkovich and Giodarno 1979; Cloward and Piven, 1979; Richards 1981; Akers, et al., 1981; Ageton 1983).

Since Simon's and Adler's works were the first major monographs on the topic, they have been particularly influential and widely cited. Both works advance a similar perspective, and it is not surprising that the two scholars eventually collaborated on a work together (Adler and Simon 1979). However, the type of theory advocated is a quite ordinary one wherein the gender differences in crime and changes in those differences are attributed to differences in the *opportunity* to commit crimes. From such a perspective females would commit more crimes if they only had the chance to do so.

Rita Simon depicts women as motivationally similar to men but inhibited from committing crimes by structured inequality. It is an extreme version of an "opportunity theory" in that she specifically argues that "Their propensities to commit crimes do not differ, but in the past their opportunities have been much more limited" (1975:47). As women move into occupational careers and economic spheres previously limited to males they allegedly have the opportunity to engage in those crimes which are facilitated by access to money and involvement in economic transactions (i.e., fraud, embezzlement, forgery and many forms of property crime).

Adler draws a similar connection between participation in legal enterprise and involvement in crime: "In the same way that women are demanding equal opportunity in fields of legitimate endeavor, a similar number of determined women are forcing their way into the world of major crimes" (1975:13). Increases in crime are interpreted as a sign of liberation: women "are cutting themselves in for a bigger piece of the pie" and making the F.B.I.'s "Most-Wanted" category is a "milestone." In short, if they had equal opportunity to engage in crime, women would do so. Women are no more moral than men, nor more concerned about suffering and harm. Rather, they have just not had the chance to be as bad as men.

It is interesting to note the similarity between these arguments and some forms of historical misogyny. Between the twelfth and seventeenth centuries thousands of people were executed for witchcraft in Europe, England and Scotland, and most estimates indicate that approximately 80 percent were women. Both Catholic and Protestant doctrines during that time depicted women as evil, deceitful, and untrustworthy. The Malleus Maleficarum, the Dominican guide for witch-hunters published in 1486, claimed that "all other wickedness is minimal" when contrasted with "the wickedness of women." This view was adopted by the new Reformation religions at the time and dramatized even more by linking reproduction to original sin. From such a perspective, were it not for constant vigilance and control of women, female deviance would run rampant. While numerous conditions combined to propagate witchhunts, the conception of women as evil has been argued to be a major reason women become the primary targets (Larner 1981: 89-102).

In Women, Crime and Criminology (1976) Carol Smart criticizes early criminologists like Lombroso and W. I. Thomas who lamented the "dangers of allowing women the same 'freedoms' as men" (71). She extends the criticism to those theorists who would attribute crime to women's emancipation as well and argues that such explanations "implicitly serve the purpose of a critique of any change in women's position" and provide "a scientistic legitimation of women's inferior social position" (76).

While Smart is critical of theories which focus on women's emancipation, she acknowledges the relevance of "role theory" to the explanation of gender differences in delinquency and states that "it is probable that the lower involvement of girls in delinquency continues to be primarily related to existing socialization patterns, in particular the greater restrictions placed on freedom of movement of most girls." (1976:68) This view is advocated with the caveat that the theory does not explain how these differences in role-related opportunity are created nor consider the impact of socioeconomic, political and historical factors on both crime and opportunity. Smart does not attempt such a task herself but merely criticizes others for not doing so.

Smart's statements were likely composed before publication of Simon's and Adler's works but do reflect the fact that some who attribute changes in female crime to opportunity, liberation, or emancipation lament that connection. However, major works by female scholars advance a similar view as a theory to be tested (Simon) or as a fact to be applauded (Adler). One side's piece of the pie may be the other's culmination of evil. To the misogynist, women would be worse than men if they could. To Simon and Adler males and females are morally and motivationally the same but vary in opportunity to commit crimes. Though there are feminist scholars who would disagree with the view that females do not differ from males in any authentically moral sense, none of those scholars are directly involved in the study of deviance.

The Critique of "Male" Methodology

The field of criminology was subjected to considerable criticism by radical and Marxist theorists during the 1970s (e.g., Quinney 1979; Taylor, Walton, and Young 1973; Krisberg 1975; Platt 1974) and the same arguments have been raised in feminist critiques of sociological (Westkott 1979: 422-430; Gould 1980: 459-467) and criminological methods (Smart 1976). The arguments raised by "new," "radical" and "critical" criminologists were directed at the conservative biases and implications of "positivism," "scientism", "casual analysis" and the research tools used in the service of science. However, such critiques said little about biases reflected in the study or neglect of women. Thus, Carol Smart (1976:183) charges both the "old" and "new" criminologies with "a total lack of awareness of the neglect of female criminality."

Smart argues that a "belief in the scientificity of positivist methodology" has produced a rift between professionals and lay persons and is geared for increasing the control that professionals exert over human lives, especially women's lives. Specifically, she posits that the adoption of a natural science methodology with its emphasis on quantification and determinism is antithetical to self-consciousness and radical change: "Within the paradigm deviant individuals are not considered to be social critics, rebels or even members of a counter-culture, rather they are treated as biological anomalies or as psychologically 'sick' individuals. Their actions are not interpreted as having a particular social significance, as being possibly rational responses, and in consequence such individuals are perceived as aberrations who must be 'cured' or removed from society." These emphases are attributed to *both* male and female sociologists and criminologists (177).

In her critique of social science methodology in general, Marcia Westkott (1979: 422-430) elaborates on several feminist and Marxist criticisms, raising issues nearly identical to those advanced by Richard Quinney (1979: 13-18) in his indictment of "the positivistic mode of inquiry" in the field of criminology. "Positivists" are depicted in both studies as committed to the search for generalizable causal relationships which are independent of time and place. Such a commitment is argued to be associated with separation of the "knower" from the "known," or a view of the subjects of research as "alien objects."

In the study of women positivism is argued to result in the casual analysis of externally determined characteristics which "can be categorized and related to one another like other phenomena" (425). Such an approach purportedly denies the "basic humanness" of the objects studied. Westkott claims that this tendency is most prominent when men study women. When women study women, on the other hand, there is a greater probability that "knowledge of the other and knowledge of self are mutually informing, because self and other share a common condition of being women" (426).

As an alternative to positivism Westkott advocates an "interpretive tradition" which "emphasizes the idea that social knowledge is always interpreted within historical contexts, and that truths are, therefore, historical rather than abstract, and contingent rather than categorical" (426). The interpretive approach, she argues, has to involve a dialogue in which meaning is discovered rather than imposed, grounded in "concrete experience rather than in abstract categories."

Westkott also claims that the positivists' search for regularities in the present through "factual recording of what is allows no justification for attending to alternatives to present conditions" and that "The effect of this approach is to justify the present" (427). She advocates social science *for* women in which the drudgery of research *about* women is accompanied by imaginative, exciting visions of alternative futures. Because action and consciousness are less likely to correspond for women than men, women's consciousness and creative imagination must be studied. The "facts" to be pursued should be those which are important to liberation.

Her concluding recommendation is for "a dialectical approach to social knowledge" which emphasizes the dialectics of: 1) self and other; 2) knowledge and practice; and 3) past and future. Such an approach is depicted as an alternative to common scientific methodology which is identified as "closed, categorical, and human-controlling."

As noted earlier, these charges and proposed alternatives are familiar to criminologists since they have been advocated in several radical critiques of criminology. However, recognizing that I may be totally blinded by years of normative socialization into the precepts of male positivism, I would like to offer a radical, dialectical defense of positivism.

Carol Smart and radical critics of criminology focus heavily on the theory and research of Cesare Lombroso and other "Italian Positivists" of the late nineteenth and early twentieth centuries. In fact, the term "positivist" is so intimately associated with Lombroso that any reference to positivism means "Italian Positivism" to most criminologists. The label stems from Lombroso's decision to pursue an explanation of crime through "the positive methods of science" as opposed to philosophical argument or deductions from basic philosophical or religious assumptions. He sought to induce generalizations from measurements of social, psychological, and physical characteristics of criminals and noncriminals and, then, to develop an interpretation of any regularities. Subsequent critics have shown much of his data to be inadequate and his interpretations to be biased. However, his efforts were sufficiently novel that most criminology texts still refer to him as the "father of scientific criminology."

Several issues must be raised in response to both Marxist and feminist critics of the "positivist mode of inquiry" or "positivist methodology." The most crucial point is that in the course of opposing the past, the evolving and dialectical nature of the positivist mode of inquiry has been ignored. Positivism is transformed into an "abstract category" and scientists become "alien objects" whose "consciousness" and basic "humanness" is denied. Scientific methodology and epistemology are not examined in their historical context but, rather, are deemed to be so inherently conservative and oppressive that they cannot be salvaged. The only solution is an alternative "interpretive," dialectical mode of inquiry.

Radical critics *define* "positivism" not as a mere commitment to identifying regularities and testing theories through the systematic collection of verifiable data but, rather, as a commitment to the status quo, a commitment to ignoring meaning and consciousness and a commitment to oppression. By doing so they ignore the uses of positivism in the pursuit of human liberation. The view that "truth" should not be a matter of authoritative declaration or purely philosophical reasoning was a revolutionary development for its time even though it may have served the interests of ruling groups. The insistence on systematic observable evidence as a requirement for differentiating myths from reality greatly expanded the prospects for challenging authority and the status quo.

The virtue of positivism is that its methodological products can and have been used to repudiate the arguments of its most avid users and to question the scientific status quo at given points in time. The liberating consequences of the positivist mode of inquiry can be found in works by the most ardent critics of positivism. Every major radical critique of criminology has applied principles of positivistic thought to criticize bad research, to identify misleading interpretations of data, and to attack myths. While "causal analysis" is attacked, principles of causal analysis (i.e., proof of association, nonspuriousness, and causal order using valid measures of variables and representative samples) are used to ferret out myths and misunderstandings. Moreover, results based on one type of systematic research are used to question conclusions based on other types of research. In the process radical critics reveal the complex and dialectical nature of science which stems from a commitment to positivism and use of its own principles against its worst proponents. Using their own terminology, such principles can be said to be one of the contradictory consequences of capitalism which originated to serve the interest of the ruling class but which changes consciousness in ways that ultimately challenge oppression. It is a positivistic assessment of the products of positivism which has enabled radical critics to attack "ruling ideas."

Finally, in proposing an "interpretive" alternative the importance of a truly dialectical methodology is actually ignored. Westkott argues, correctly, that a commitment to presupposed abstract categories and measurement of external properties is not only limiting but oppressively constraining. An intimate interpretive dialogue between the knower and the known is the likely source of new understanding and the assessment of hidden dimensions of consciousness and imagination. However, the instant that claims are made about "women" or "men," about gaps between consciousness and action, about alternatives which will have the desired consequences for women, then a critical thinker will ask questions about generalizability, representativeness, causation, bias, validity and the whole range of issues generated by positivists.

Through interpretive, humanistic scholarship and qualitative methods new ideas are generated and we change our minds about what is known and what it is that we want to know. Yet, it is inevitable that we will also want to know whether ideas are idiosyncratic, whether imaginations are constrained, whether there are variations in consciousness, what form they take, and how they change. In the process of pursuing answers we will worry about discerning order and patterns which go beyond the subjects we have consulted. We will want to identify the external properties of the world around them which shaped their thinking and their actions and which currently preclude certain futures. Once we begin thinking about such questions we are likely to turn to existing tools for discerning order in large samples or populations such as social surveys and structured interviews. We will want to measure structure, consciousness and action to discern the reciprocal or causal relationships among them. We adopt a positivistic mode of thought because the pursuit of understanding involves several styles of thought. In fact, I am willing to propose that the most liberating social science is likely to be a product of both traditions.

Some Basic Issues and Their Relevance to Deviance

In 1975, when the first issue of the journal *Signs* was published, its editor identified it as a vehicle for disseminating the best in the new scholarship about women. Similarly, a special issue of *Social Problems* was published in 1976 devoted exclusively to "feminist perspectives." The exact parameters of the new scholarship on women have not, and probably cannot, be *completely* specified. When there was virtually no literature specifically about women, merely dealing with the topic might qualify a work as part of that new field. However, as more and more literature appears and the mission of feminist scholars succeeds, the new scholarship loses some of its novelty. Yet, there is one characteristic that the most applauded feminist literature shares and which is recent enough to justify attributions of novelty: it identifies and elaborates on the relevance of gender to basic assumptions underlying philosophical, metaphysical, and scientific thought-assumptions which have been taken for granted by predominantly male scholars (e.g., "rationality," "morality," "objectivity," and "justice").

While such issues are raised by scholars who are not specifically interested in deviance, the issues raised should appear especially relevant to sociologists interested in gender and deviance. Certain questions immediately come to mind when the relevance of gender to such philosophical issues is considered. If "rationality" is more characteristic of males than females, then why do males engage in so many more destructive activities than females? If males are better able to evaluate situations unemotionally and "objectively," then why should such assessments lead them to attack themselves, their loved ones and the world around them so much more frequently than females? If the great advances in moral reasoning and justice are male accomplishments and males are better able to adjudicate among competing rights, then why are males more likely than females to ignore rights, to violate moral standards, and to be responsible for so much more injustice? Knowledge of gender differences in deviance should reinforce dissatisfaction with common stereotypes.

Concepts such as rationality, objectivity, and justice all have positive connotations; that is, we tend to view then as "good," as something to be valued, as traits to be encouraged for the benefit of human progress, whereas the most prominent and eminently sociological theories of deviance have viewed male deviance as either "good" behavior or "rational," "just" and "normal" responses to circumstances beyond their control.

If we examine the arguments of the most prominent deviance theorists of the twentieth century—Robert Merton and Edwin

Sutherland—we find that they both view crime as either moral and normative or rational behavior, a product of man's most uniquely social and human qualities. Robert Merton begins his classic essay "Social Structure and Anomie" by challenging "The image of man as an untamed bundle of impulses" and proposes a theory wherein "infringement of social codes constitutes a 'normal' (that is to say, an expected) response" (1968: 185). In his theory crime becomes a reasonable response to restricted opportunity in a sociocultural system stressing "success." Such structural-cultural strain generates "intense pressure for deviation." One response to such pressure is crime, which Merton views as a form of "innovation"; that is, when legitimate avenues to success are limited and emphasis on success is strong, people will adopt or create innovative means of accomplishing the same ends. Thus, many forms of crime are translated into rational, problem-solving responses to structural strain.

In another classic (*Delinquency and Opportunity* 1960) Richard Cloward and Lloyd Ohlin add two ideas to Merton's theory. They argue that the form of the response depends on the criminal and delinquent organizations or traditions already available in a person's immediate social environment. Furthermore, they stress that it is when people develop a "sense of indignation about their disadvantages" and ascribe their failures "to injustice in the social system" that the response is likely to be directed outward in the form of criminal or delinquent behavior. Thus, while Merton created an image of crime as a rational response to social conditions, Cloward and Ohlin transform criminal conduct into a response which is "justified" by social injustice. Rather than being irrational or impulsive, delinquency is viewed as a normal response by rational beings. Rather than stressing the injustice of the crime, Cloward and Ohlin represent the offender as the victim of injustice and his behavior as an innovative resolution to structural injustice. Behavior typically seen as irrational and unjust becomes a positive response to irrationality and injustice in the social system.

Edwin Sutherland and Donald Cressey (1974) and other cultural deviance theorists (see Miller 1958) accomplish the same transformation in a different way. While rejecting the view that delinquency is an instrumental response to specific status problems they transform deviant behavior into conforming behavior. Immoral conduct from the perspective of some segments of society becomes moral conduct from other perspectives. People become criminal or delinquent because the cultural standards they learn are in conflict with the standards reflected in the law. Advocating such an interpretation, Walter Miller (1958) argues that lower-class gang members "possess to an unusually high degree both the *capacity* and the *motivation* to conform to perceived cultural norms." It just happens that those norms call for or justify behavior which conflicts with the law. In sum, deviance is transformed into conformity, bad conduct into good conduct and injustice into justice.

What does this digression into criminological theory have to do with the new scholarship for or about women? It points to a tendency in dealing with a predominantly "male" form of behavior to transform it in ways which make it appear to be "good." In most areas of sociology the study of male-female differences involves accomplishments which are generally valued, such as achievement, occupational success, inventiveness, creativity and scientific progress. In the sociology of deviance the differences observed could be interpreted as "bad," as "costly," and "undesirable." Yet, they are not. Behavior which appears destructive becomes constructive. Behavior which appears irrational becomes rational. Behavior which appears to be unjust toward others becomes an attempt to establish justice. Deviant behavior becomes an achievement, a form of success, a creative invention or a moral accomplishment.

Yet, it appears as a strange sort of rationality when the facts about crime are considered. Since the characteristics of offenders correspond with the characteristics of victims for many forms of crime, then we would have to conclude that offenders are "innovatively" destroying themselves. If crime is socially approved conduct in distinct subcultures, then members of such subcultures appear to be working to destroy their own communities. It is a strange morality that can survive when its strongest advocates are also its most likely victims. If crime is a response to injustice, then how can the redistribution of further injustice to fellow travelers do anything more than compound the problem? While I certainly do not expect people to ask these questions when contemplating criminal choices, it is not unreasonable to expect that sociologists should justify their imagery of crime by more precisely specifying the sense in which criminal behavior is moral, innovative, just, and rational.

While deviance theorists have not pursued concepts such as justice and rationality in detail, processes of "justice reasoning" have been central to works by cognitive psychologists. One of the most prominent of these, Lawrence Kohlberg (1969; 1971; 1981; Kohlberg, Levine, and Hewer 1983) has spent years researching such reasoning. Using hypothetical dilemmas where property rights conflict with the right to life, Kohlberg reports that there is an orderly structure to justice reasoning which parallels cognitive development. At the highest stages of moral development people weigh conflicting rights and reach decisions which are justified by general principles involving a hierarchy of rights. Thus, in circumstances where basic needs are not being met by a social system, criminal choices could be interpreted as attempts to establish justice.

Kohlberg is careful to note that he is studying moral *reasoning* and not moral *action*. In fact, in his most recent work he notes that the relation between moral action and moral reasoning should be a central issue for further theory and research. Hence, the fact that a person would recommend stealing to resolve a moral dilemma and, then, justify that choice by referring to a hierarchy of rights does not mean that he would do so in real life. It is the *justice reasoning* or the form of *justification*, that, Kohlberg argues follows an increasingly universalistic and general developmental sequence. In fact, in response to critics who argue that his theory implies that "liberalism" is inevitable, Kohlberg and his colleagues state that their "meta-ethical assumptions" about development in terms of increasing universality and reversability of general principles can be embraced without presuming that they lead to any particular normative or moral position; that is, developmental sequences can be studied regardless of the actual *moral content* of such reasoning or its relation to actual moral action.

Carol Gilligan (1977; 1981) has criticized Kohlberg for focusing so heavily on the rational, calculative, weighting, and balancing of rights as the central property of mature moral reasoning and argues that there is also a structural sequence to the development of other ethical principles governing choice. Whereas males at the most mature levels of judgment may use general principles of "justice" wherein conflicting abstract rights are adjudicated, females accord primacy to generalized principles of care, responsibility and sacrifice. She is especially critical of Kohlberg's (1969; 1971; 1981) theory of justice reasoning because it implies that women are less likely than men to advance to the most morally mature and universalistic stages of reasoning.

Kohlberg has responded to Gilligan by arguing that there are few sex differences in justice reasoning and any differences observed are likely to be products of other variables (e.g., education) or the nature of the moral dilemma (public versus private) presented. Moreover, he argues that "We see justice as both rational *and* implying an attitude of empathy" (Kohlberg, Levine, and Hewer 1983:24) and that "many moral situations or dilemmas do not pose a choice between one or the other orientation" (134). At the advanced "postconventional" stages the two orientations converge. Both the justice ethic and the care ethic are viewed as reflecting a sense of universal bonds and connectedness to others. At postconventional levels "justice concerns lose their retributive and rule bound nature for the sake of treating persons as person; i.e., as ends in themselves. This principle is common to both the ethic of care and the ethic of justice" (137).

Kohlberg's response has interesting but unrecognized implications, as did his earlier depictions of the highest stages of moral judgment. At such stages justice is defined as a universalistic "respect for people" (1981: 40) and involves a commitment of "human rights" allegedly applied without regard for national, local, or self interests. If such principles are evidence of moral maturity, then Kohlberg's theory implies that *females are more likely to operate at his integrated "postconventional" stages than are males.* Jerald Bachman, Lloyd Johnston and Patrick O'Malley have been gathering data from a nationally representative sample of high school seniors since 1975 and publish the questionnaire responses by sex, race, region, college plans and illicit drug use each year. A wide range of questions have been asked about values, attitudes and beliefs. Their data shows that females express more sympathy toward starving people in other nations and are more willing to personally sacrifice something to help them, more willing to contribute to the life of the poor and feel they could get along with much less if it would help (Bachman et al., 1980: 179-180). Females exhibit a far wider range of bonds to more different people and with greater intensity than do males. Males indicate a greater willingness to go to war than females while females exhibit greater support for unilateral disarmament.

It is clear that female empathy, a sense of care, responsibility, and sacrifice are not merely principles applied at the private, particularistic level but extend beyond immediate relationships to encompass people in general. The data could be used to argue that males have a less generalized concern for the happiness of others than females and are more likely to make decisions which maintain existing societal, group, or individual privilege.

These findings are consistent with Gilligan's depiction of female morality and with arguments by Nancy Chodorow concerning the *Reproduction of Mothering* (1978). Chodorow argues that boys are pushed or eased out of a close relation with their mothers and encouraged to develop their own autonomous and separate identities. In modern society the world they encounter and help reproduce is one in which status is determined by physical prowess, money, competitive success, or position whether in the world of peers or the adult world. Girls, on the other hand, experience greater continuity, less autonomy and less separation. They define themselves and their location in the world in relational terms. They are taught to care and to share. Since principles of "need" are more likely to be emphasized for allocating resources in the family than in the public economy, girls are likely to develop a commitment to what appears to be "socialistic" or "liberal" principles. In contrast, allocation of resources based on power and competitive success is not only expected in a boy's world but is reinforced by a capitalist economy. Experience in the struggle for power and success and security in competitive peer group relationships are good preparation for success in capitalist enterprises. Both worlds are filled with competition, conflict, and insecurity and this is the "expected" state of affairs for males. As Gilligan notes, the male imagery of the world is one of "dangerous confrontation and explosive connection" (1982: 38). This tendency appears even in men's stories involving intimate relationships. It is a world in which "connection is fragmental and communication fails." While this depiction is based on clinical cases and small samples, it is perfectly consistent with years of research on delinquent gangs (Jansyn 1968; Yablonsky 1959; Klein and Crawford 1967; Bordua 1962).

Gilligan, Chodorow and other female scholars have been moving us toward a more conscious recognition of different conceptions of rationality, impartiality, objectivity, and justice but have not challenged prevailing notions as much as they actually could. For example, it could have been proposed that there are two conceptions of justice rather than an ethic of care *versus* justice. Males tend to conceive of justice reasoning as an impartial application of rules which is facilitated by emotional distance and objectivity. Females tend to conceive of justice reasoning as an impartial attempt to meet human needs which is facilitated by a generalized love for others. The former is no more "impartial" than the latter and no more "rational." It may be more "objective" in the sense that the issues to be adjudicated involve competing, autonomous "objects" inevitably conflicting with each other in the pursuit of self-interest, but this conception is more of a *description* of the male world than a statement of what a just world would be like.

Conclusions

This review of the literature encountered in my mainstreaming efforts was designed to highlight those arguments which I believe will generate intellectual excitement among sociologists interested in deviance. Some arguments in major works by women scholars, including feminist scholars, are not likely to generate new discoveries or insights because they merely apply old theories or because they ignore authentically positive and moral characteristics of the female world.

Westkott's arguments that a social science *for* women, with women studying women, will be more liberating than one *about* women involving male and female scholars contradicts her own observations concerning the image of "woman." She states that from a feminist view "masculinity and femininity are simply different human possibilities that have emerged historically" (1979: 424). If this observation is to contribute as much to understanding society and people as Westkoff maintains, then it necessitates a study of *gender similarities and differences* in historical context. The study of the female world provides a contrast for understanding the male world and the study of the male world provides a valuable contrast for understanding the female world. In developing her feminist social science as proposed, Westkott is as likely to advance stereotypical, abstract models of the male world as males have generated by ignoring or stereotyping the female world.

Westkott shows no more familiarity with the diversity of the male world and the diverse imaginations of alternative futures among males than the sexist scholars she indicts. She reifies and objectifies "masculinity" to the point that it is no longer a historically specific variation in human possibilities but a negative stereotype for defining woman. She stresses female alienation in a man-made world allegedly characterized by a happy compatibility of culture and personality. Yet, man's alienation from his own world is central to male social science as well and the "happy" compatible relationship between capitalist "culture" and the male personality has not made us all as happy as she thinks. If crime is linked to that compatibility, then it costs us a great deal.

I have argued that research on gender differences inevitably requires both positivistic and interpretive techniques. For every instance where "positivism" has defended the status quo, one can find another instance where its products have been the basis for challenging it. Moreover, not only are positivistic norms crucial to all radical critiques of prior theory and research, but research has been the basis for challenging the very stereotypes which critics blame on positivism. It is scholars more committed to theory and precedent than to proof that mislead us the most, and the positivistic mode of thinking has been indispensible for identifying when we are most likely to be misled.

The tendency to applaud female crime as an indicator of liberation or to attribute it to progress in economic opportunity transforms female crime in the same way male criminologists transformed male crime. Bad behavior becomes an accomplishment and variations in what might appear to be virtue become mere variations in structural constraints. Yet, when we read Gilligan, Chodorow (and other authors such as Jessie Bernard, The Female World, 1981) there are differences which seem to go beyond current constraints, reflecting a history of limitations and/or something enduring and positive about the female world. A conscious recognition of positive values associated with "femininity" might suppress violence even if every woman were handed a gun. Justice sounds different when discussed by women. Sacrifice somehow sounds rational and purposive. "Peace" carries connotations of harmony generated by connectedness and fulfillment of basic needs in contrast to a balance of power among autonomous beings or nations.

By emphasizing the possibility that the low female crime rate reflects something positive about women, we should be careful not to construct a totally negative, contrary view of the male world. While there are differences between males and females in the aggregate, there is considerable overlap. Differences in morality are statistically significant but do not show the majority of males to be insensitive, selfish opportunists. Moreover, the same surveys which show females to exhibit a more universalistic concern for human needs also show that males are significantly more likely to indicate they would take action to protest social issues (Bachman et al. 1980). While Gilligan would argue that such differences reflect educational socialization where girls are taught to be passive it is also possible that passivity may be a correlated dimension of a value system emphasizing nonviolence, sacrifice, sharing, and love. It is ironic that the sex most likely to act tends to exhibit more parochial and self-interested ethics while the sex with the more universalistic ethical system is quiet about it. But, it is also worthy to note that when the two tendencies have converged in the active but nonviolent pursuit of justice based on shared connectedness, both men and women have succeeded in bringing about major social change.

References

Adler, Freda. 1975. *Sisters in Crime*. New York: McGraw-Hill.

————, and Rita Simon. 1979. *The Criminology of Deviant Women*. Boston: Houghton Mifflin Company.

Ageton, Suzanne S. 1983. "The Dynamics of Female Delinquency, 1976-1980." *Criminology* 21 (November): 555-584.

Akers, Ronald L., Marvin D. Krohn, Marcia Radosevich and Lonn Lanza-Kaduce. 1981. "Social Characteristics and Self-reported Delinquency: Differences in Extreme Types." In *The Sociology of Delinquency*. Gary F. Jensen (ed.) pp. 29-48. Beverly Hills: Sage Publications.

Bachman, J., J. Johnston and P. O'Malley. 1980. *Monitoring the Future*. Ann Arbor, Michigan: Institute for Social Research.

Bernard, Jesse. 1981. *The Female World*. New York: The Free Press.

Boals, Kay. 1975. "The Politics of Male-female Relations: The Functions of Feminist Scholarship." *Signs* 1 (Autumn): 161-174.

Bordua, David J. 1962. "Some Comments of Theories of Group Delinquency." *Sociological Inquiry* 32: 245-260.

Bowker, Lee H. 1978. *Women, Crime and the Criminal Justice System*. Lexington, Mass.: Lexington Books, D.C. Health and Company.

Cernkovich, Stephen A., and Peggy C. Giodarno. 1979. "A Comparative Analysis of Male and Female Delinquency." *The Sociological Quarterly* 20 (Winter): 131-145.

Chodorow, Nancy. 1978. *The Reproduction of Mothering: Psychoanalysis and the Sociology of Gender*. Berkeley: University of California Press.

Cloward, Richard A., and Frances Fox Piven. 1979. "Hidden Protest: The Channeling of Female Innovation and Resistance." *Signs* 4 (November): 651-669.

Cloward, Richard, and Lloyd Ohlin. 1960. *Delinquency and Opportunity*. Glencoe, Illinois: The Free Press.

Datesman, Susan K., and Frank R. Scarpittiz (eds.). 1980. *Women, Crime and Justice*. New York: Oxford University Press.

Gilligan, Carol. 1977. "In a Different Voice: Women's Conception of the Self and Morality." *Harvard Educational Review* 47 (4), November: 481-517.

———, 1981. "Moral Development in the College Years." In *The Modern American College*. A. Chickering (ed.). San Francisco: Jossey Bass, pp. 139-157.

———, 1982. *In a Different Voice: Psychological Theory and Women's Development*. Cambridge, Mass.: Harvard University Press.

Gould, Meridith. 1980. "The New Sociology." *Signs* 5 (No. 3): 459-467.

Harris, Anthony R. 1977. "Sex and Theories of Deviance." *American Sociological Review* 42 (February): 3-16.

Jansyn, L. R. 1968. "Solidarity and Delinquency in a Street Corner Group." *American Sociological Review* 21: 600-614.

Jensen, Gary F., and Dean G. Rojek. 1980. *Delinquency: A Sociological View*. Lexington, Mass.: D.C. Health and Company.

Jensen, Gary F., and Raymond Eve. 1976. "Sex Differences in Delinquency: An Examination of Popular Sociological Explanations." *Criminology* 13 (February): 427-448.

Klein, Malcolm, and L. Y. Crawford. 1967. "Groups, Gangs and Cohesiveness." *Research in Crime and Delinquency* 4: 63-75.

Kohlberg, L. 1969. "Stage and Sequence: The Cognitive Development

Approach to Socialization." In *Handbook of Socialization Theory and Research*. D.A. Goslin (ed.). Chicago: Rand McNally.

_____, 1971. "From Is to Ought: How to Commit the Naturalistic Fallacy and Get Away with It in the Study of Moral Development." in *Cognitive Development and Epistemology*. T. Mischel (ed.) pp. 151-235. New York: Academic Press.

_____, 1981. *Essays in Moral Development*. Vols. 1 and 2. New York: Harper Row.

_____, and C. Gilligan. 1971. "The Adolescent as a Philosopher: The Discovery of the Self in a Post-conventional World." *Daedalus* 100 (4): 1051-1086.

_____, Levine, C., and A. Hewer. 1983. *Moral Stages: A Current Reformulation and Response to Critics*. New York: Karger.

Krisberg, Barry. 1975. *Crime and Privilege: Toward a New Criminology*. Englewood Cliffs, New Jersey: Prentice-Hall, Inc.

Larner, Christina. 1981. *Enemies of God*. New York: The New York Public Library and Arno Press, Inc.

Merton, Robert K. 1968. *Social Theory and Social Structure*. Glencoe, Illinois: Free Press.

Miller, Walter. 1958. "Lower Class Culture as a Generating Milieu of Gang Delinquency." *Journal of Social Issues* 14: 5-19.

Platt, Tony. 1974. "Prospects for a Radical Criminology in the United States." *Crime and Social Justice* 1 (Spring-Summer): 2-10.

Quinney, Richard. 1979. *Criminology*. Boston: Little, Brown and Company.

Richards, Pamela. 1981. "Quantitative and Qualitative Sex Differences in Middle-class Delinquency." *Criminology* 18 (February): 453-470.

Schur, Edwin M. 1984. *Labeling Women Deviant*. New York: Random House.

Simon, Rita. 1975. *Women and Crime*. Lexington, Mass.: D.C. Health and Company.

Smart, Carol. 1976. *Women, Crime and Criminology: A Feminist Critique*. London: Routledge and Kegan Paul Ltd.

Steffensmeier, Darrell J., and Renee Hoffman Steffensmeier. 1980. "Trends in Female Delinquency: An Examination of Arrest, Juvenile Court, Self-report and Field Data." *Criminology* 18: 62-85.

Stimpson, Catharine R., Joan N. Burstyn, Donna C. Stanton and Sandra M. Whisler. 1975. "Editorial." *Signs* 1 (Autumn): v-viii.

Sutherland, Edwin H., and Donald R. Cressey. 1974. *Criminology*. Ninth Edition. Philadelphia: J. B. Lippincott.

Taylor, Ian, Paul Walton and Jock Young. 1973. *The New Criminology*. New York: Harper and Row Publishers.

Warren, Marguerite. 1981. *Comparing Male and Female Offenders*. Beverly Hills, California: Sage Publications.

Weisberg, D. Kelly (ed.). 1982. *Women and the Law*. Cambridge, Massachusetts: Schenkman.

Weis, Joseph G. 1976. "Liberation and Crime: The Invention of the New Female Criminal." *Crime and Social Justice* 6 (Fall-Winter): 17-27.

Westkott, Marcia. 1979. "Feminist Criticism of the Social Sciences." *Harvard Educational Review* 49 (November): 422-430.

Yablonsky, Lewis. 1959. "The Delinquent Gang as a Near-group." *Social Problems* 7 (Fall): 108-17.

6. Teaching the Politics of Gender in Literature: Two Proposals for Reform, With a Reading of Hamlet

I

As the redoubtable *Newsweek* would have it, the mainstreaming of women's issues and women's writing into university courses on literature means "adding female authors to [class] reading lists" and is therefore "easy enough" for instructors who know the requisite books and poems.[1] Such a method, alongside separate courses on women in Western thought, is indeed fairly common nationwide when literature faculties make any effort at all to deal with the new scholarship on women. Still, like the notion of a segregated course, this recipe is a resistance to full-scale change. It almost invariably says "mix, but don't stir"; it assumes that there are "women's concerns" within the spheres and writings of women that need to be addressed but need not necessarily touch or alter the spheres and concerns of men. If a professor of literature teaching a survey course, say, shifts (as I once did) to the problem of female identity only in *Wuthering Heights* (often the token piece by a woman author in a survey of British literature), Catherine Earnshaw's fragmentation by male-dominated and male-serving models for female behavior[2] can easily seem an isolated phenomenon, an aberration in the works of the "great literary canon." Other books in the course, and even parts of Emily Bronte's centered on men alone, can remain divorced from the issue of gender restrictions as though such boundary lines affect only women or, for that matter, only some women characters in some books by some women authors. How can such an approach make any claim to validity? Even average students, women *and* men, can and do see this assumption as a cowardly dodge that avoids what some of them know already: how pervasive gender limits are in the ways we are urged to form our "identities." Moreover, for those students who somehow ignore these facts of life, there is still the problem of focussing on sexual inequality only when the "woman's book" is being discussed. That focus seems a jarring intrusion of "political" issues into what should be a purely conceptual or aesthetic course, since many students (like many of their instructors) still assume that the realms of literature and politics are separate. Techniques in art, supposedly, have little to do with structures of power in Western society.

I would argue that genuine "mainstreaming" happens—though I would prefer to call it a recovery of the undercurrent, a return of the repressed—when the parameters and the politics of gender become central problems in every text taught, whatever the era and whoever the author. Gender, as we know, is not identical to sex but is rather a linguistic-rhetorical-ideological construct ("man" or "woman") attached to people by social convention as one result of sex. This "socially defined portraiture," in the words of Erving Goffman, though "no more 'natural' and inevitable than [an] occupational role," operates as a given "anchoring of activity," a grounding of a person's potentials in a limited set of permitted qualities and acts.[3] The limits are prescribed by what Michel Foucault has called the hegemonic "grids of intelligibility" in the "social order" of the moment. These grids are the temporary products or projections of interdependent social groups (gender groups such as "men" coupled with such socioeconomic groups as "hunters," "owners," "clergy," or "aristocrats") that have gained enough dominance in the social division of labor to dictate the functions of the signs and metaphors that people use to conceive of, and so to *produce*, themselves.[4] Gender, then, constructed and imposed in this way, helps determine the spaces or modes of action into which human tendencies can be "deployed"[5] and thereby circumscribed within "appropriate" masculine and feminine ways of being. Gender is a conscription of persons into a kind of dictionary, a part of the naming process after birth, a mode of production *and* definition specifying which avenues are open and which are closed to different groups of people.

I cannot think of a character or speaker in a literary work—be it among the canonized "classics" or one of those pieces now

marginalized in the male-centered curriculum—who does not confront this alienation of personality into a gender-divided discourse.
More than any other beings, such figures are obviously created in,
deployed by, and conscripted within the marketplace of linguistic-
symbolic options channeling the confusion of human inclinations
into what it is properly "masculine" or "effeminate" to do, possess,
be, or desire. Take, for example, the many struggles within himself
verbalized by one of the best-known of literary characters: Shakespeare's Hamlet. He feels he must stage his personality in aggressive,
"masculine" ways so that he can beat down the incongruities in his
bodily sensations, his conflicting patterns of thought and emotion,
and his language, replete as it is with disruptive punnings and plays
between different words and their multiple meanings. The cultural
discourse in which he must fashion a "self," after all, defines such
feelings and tangles as "but foolery," the "kind of gainsgiving as
would perhaps trouble a woman" (*Hamlet, Prince of Denmark*,
V.ii.204-05).[6] Throughout Western literature, characters or speakers, all of them beginning with that very human sense of division
within themselves, are similarly wrenched outward and culturally
positioned in impossibly neat gender oppositions by forced divisions of humankind in the discourse frames that control authors,
and hence their creations, to an astonishing degree.

Clearly, unless we study how gender-based designations and
repressions limit writers, characters, and modes of description, we
cannot grasp larger issues: how a culturally determined "style makes
the man" or the woman in a text and a social arena; how that
distinction is used to drain power from the members of one gender
into those of another; and how or why the consequent array of
human possibilities and restrictions is imaged or shaped the way it is
in literature as we have it. To discuss the governing principles of texts
in the classroom without revealing these drives as among the most
basic in each work is simply to avoid the truth about how texts
operate and what forces have impinged upon them. For the sake of
fundamental accuracy, then, standard literature courses should
concern themselves with analyzing how texts, whether male- or
female-authored, stylize and configure gender-enforcing divisions as
these dichotomies battle the personal, social, and linguistic tendencies that try to resist them.

Yet what must actually occur, one might ask, in the daily
conduct and practical organization of such a reconstituted literature

class? There are, I think, both some reasonably obvious and some more far reaching, more basic answers to this question. Obviously, as feminist critics have argued, the whole notion of what is "mainstream" or "canonical" must be put in question when texts are chosen.[7] We should teach more texts by and about women, especially ones that stylishly and powerfully address the ways that our otherness-from-ourselves *within* ourselves is deployed by systems of symbols into the Standard Gender and the "other sex" of male-female distinctions. To that end we must often dismantle the frequent exclusion from "literariness" of the diary, the journal, the confession, the prose epistle, the essay, and the poem or play that crosses official generic boundaries.[8] Further, when we retain canonized texts for study we must continually point to their procedures for channeling character potentials into gendered types. Such a focus will reveal what texts really do to resist or succumb to this drive toward distortion. What is not precisely gendered *nor* officially generic will thus be brought to the foreground as never before, deepening our understanding of the complex "classics of Western thought."[9]

Such strategies are most effective, moreover, when the course has a theme or general focus requiring their use, as I have discovered repeatedly in revising many "core-curriculum" survey courses on the history of Western culture or the development of English literature. I find that deployment by gender appears just as important as other fundamental tendencies in the works only when I present the chosen texts as responses to common problems or concerns from which the gender system is inseparable. For me it is especially helpful in historical surveys of literature to predefine the successive writers as dealing, under changing economic and ideological pressures, with the human need to seek or construct a sense of identity, a place in the larger structure of the social and natural world, as each writer fashions it out of the linguistic context in his or her historical moment. Literature, as I ask the students to see it, exists in part to configure this constitutive process attempted by, or imposed upon, every person in history, especially since that process parallels the author's hypothetical constructions of characters, voices, and even "authority" in a detailed patterning of already textualized experience. A focus on this formative effort, this emergence of "self" into and out of public and symbolic patterns, can easily make the students observe—since gender is one of the basic symbolic orders into which the subject emerges—the process determining so-called "sexual identity" throughout a particular text. If the object of study in this literature course is thus defined, students can see the self in any text as primarily the product of linguistic and social conventions that try to en-gender that self from the start.

At the same time, for true revision, these relatively simple changes are inadequate if they are neither developed further nor allowed to rest on any deeper assumptions. There are many potential problems that could arise if the above suggestions were implemented just as they stand. Such a gender-focused and thematic approach could, for example, risk making every text say the same thing. The class might increasingly overlook the very different styles of gender distinction in different authors, the different preconceptions of these authors that the styles guide and express, and the culture-specific, time-specific political and ideological forces that draw all authors toward their special assumptions about the structure of the world and the placement of beings within it. Proponents of such a course might also fail to see that it may be doing what its exclusionary predecessors have done. It may be drawing students toward a particular, limited sense of literature (since all senses must be momentary and incomplete) without acknowledging either the provisionality of that view or the students' right to know the temporary assumptions behind it. Moreover, the theme of variations on identity construction, because there is a oneness implied in the very term "identity," can also lead a student to assume that rigidly stable identities should be made to exist—and in ways that could restore a binary opposition between genders that would restrict human potential once again.

Consequently, though I do urge the fairly easy revisions I have listed above, I mainly want to offer two further, more far reaching proposals that may prevent the evasions just noted. The first suggests a series of steps for analyzing texts in class, steps whose validity I want to demonstrate by filling out my reading of *Hamlet*, one of those "classic" texts most likely to escape this revisionary mode of reading. These steps should help students connect the power dynamics of gender distinctions with several other aspects of a text: the most basic assumptions in an author's style, his or her structuring of self-other relations, and his or her negotiation between the ideologies available at the time the work was produced. My second proposal articulates a possible redefinition of "literature" to be assumed by all the readings in the sort of revised survey that I have already suggested. Such a reorientation of what a text is perceived to be and do should reconstitute the focus of literary study and thereby make gender issues fundamental to the teaching and analysis of literature in the university. I propose to spell out these two suggestions one at a time, as they might be (or, in my case, have been) pursued in an undergraduate course on the quest for identity in Western literature.

II

My first idea asks students to start each analysis with a probe that initially seems to sideline gender. It urges them to ferret out in each text the deepest underlying assumptions of how an "identity" of *any* sort is conceivable, or hard to conceive, within the various relationships among the elements making up the hypothetical "world-order" of the piece. At the very beginning, of course, the students must be given some sense of the several existing verbal constructs ("sources") or concepts of identity *prior* to the work, concepts which the author seeks to recombine and revise. Then they should be asked to consider the known pressures affecting the revision at that historical moment—the economic exchange systems, the classes of people within those systems, the separate ideological formations emerging from among those separate classes,[10] the author's affiliations with one or more classes and ideologies—all of which are produced by rivalries between social groups, and therefore between conflicting manners of perception, as the society of that era (like all societies) undergoes a transition between different social orders. At this point the students should see how the making of any "identical" formation, be it a coherent text or a character in it, has to be an attempt at unifying a cacophony of social and linguistic differences (including different symbolizings of a person's nature). This cacophony can only seem to become harmonious in a concealment of differences behind temporarily dominant ideologies that organize how the world, society, and the individual are constituted. The presuppositions in any depicted search for identity, then, must either expose or try to suppress—and thus reveal by suppressing—schisms in the modes of thinking and acting used by a certain age to deal with social change and yet to articulate self-

definitions at the same time. Students should finally see the quest for
identity represented in a given text as a power play where different
ideologies of human being are forced into an attempted concord
working to overcome an ever-present discord.[11]

Shakespeare's Prince of Denmark begins *The Tragedy of Hamlet*
in this very state of self-division, mainly because of conflicts in
ideology permeating the Renaissance England of 1600. Such a
schism is quite evident in the Prince's early and famous analogy
between the body politic of Claudius' Denmark and the body of any
person corrupted by "the stamp of one defect" (I. iv. 31). On the
one hand, the source of the defect in both "bodies" is an accident of
birth, the "stamp" of the "mole . . . Being nature's livery, or
fortune's star" (I. v. 31, 24, and 32). This possibility recalls an
aristocratic ideology that would base behavioral tendencies on what
is predetermined by one's birth into a certain class (with appropriate
"livery") or one's emergence at the time of a certain stellar
configuration. Be it a blood inheritance or a dictate from the fates, a
person in this scheme must enact an ancestral demand written on the
"book and volume of [his] brain" in a way appropriate to his station
as heir (I. v. 103), as Hamlet later claims he must do when he is
enjoined by his father's ghost to be the "scourge and minister" of
"heaven" (III. iv. 174-76). On the other hand, the predestined
"dram of evil" brings the whole body's "substance" to "scandal"
only if it leads, as have Claudius' revels, to the body being "traduced
and taxed" in the eyes of others (I. iv. 38 and 18). Contesting the
purely aristocratic line is the more early bourgeois notion of
Renaissance "rhetorical man," the ideology suggesting that a person
fashions his character over time by persuasive techniques given their
status, not by his past, but by his audience.[12] This styling of the self
could hardly have escaped Shakespeare's attention, since he, like
other knowing exploiters of "Renaissance self-fashioning," was a
self-made son of middle class parents, one who aimed for a coat of
arms, royal patronage, and thus a courtly audience in the capacity of
rhetorician, playwright, actor, and entrepreneur pretending to be
many other "selves."[13]

Hamlet is plainly caught in the crossfire of these different
stances. If a man is the sheer inheritor of a blood-code, there need be
no real division between motive and action. Upon hearing the ghost
tell of the "Murder most foul," Hamlet can, by his own account,
begin at once to "sweep to [his] revenge" (I. v. 31). Yet if all

performances are other than they seem, if motive is in fact hidden or transmuted on its way to an enactment that seeks only the spectator's granting of power to a mere actor, then the ghost may be a deception having but "power/T'assume a pleasing shape" (II. ii. 582-83). There may be no ordained motive for action at all, and the grounds for action can only come from an audience response forcing an actor to react appropriately, as when Hamlet reacts to the posture of Claudius after the usurper has seen the Prince's play-within-the-play. The Amleth of Saxo Grammaticus, Shakespeare's oldest source for *Hamlet*, does not have this problem because he accepts the aristocratic blood-code without question and needs only to find deceptive ways to circumvent the watchfulness of the usurper king's bodyguard.[14] The blocks to Hamlet's revenge are more psychological, not just because Claudius now has no bodyguard, but because these impediments are basic to the ideological conflict out of which the Prince forms his theory of self and action. Torn between a oneness of motive with action and a wide breach between the two, he becomes "unpregnant of [his] cause" (II. ii. 553), and, if he is to act as he is bidden to do, he must fashion or stage a *rapprochement* between these two positions, using whatever rhetorical or cultural means will allow him to maintain both ideologies and yet heal the conflict by suppressing one beneath the other.

The first step in Hamlet's solution is fairly easy to find, but it cannot finally grant him the transcendence of conflict that he needs to attain some mastery over the language schemes that initially master him. What aristocratic and rhetorical man seem to share most in the authorized depictions of both, indeed what makes the "sins of [or against] the fathers" be "visited upon the sons" *and* the figure of man be divided between appearance and hidden reality, is the Christian conception of the Fall that sees every postlapserian kingdom or soul as a "rank" and "unweeded garden," an Eden corrupted, fallen away from a desired level that "knows not 'seems' " into a state where "forms, moods, griefs" do not "denote [one] truly" yet remain all we have to go on in human relations (I. ii. 135-36 and 76-82). Consequently Hamlet embraces this widely serviceable rhetoric right from the first line of his first soliloquy, finding in Original Sin (and one in particular) the reason why his kingdom and his "time [are] out of joint" and so proceeding to ferret out the ironic duplicities in nearly every person, action, discourse, or appearance of virtue. With the help of this way of seeing, he at least becomes a "scourge and minister" in the sense that he satirizes the pretensions of almost everyone at court throughout Acts II to IV. He plays the palace fool in the absence of an official one and so reveals in the language of Elsinore double entendres exposing the corruption—the decentered play of appearances crafting postures powerful enough to overcome their rivals—that pervades the court, the kingdom, humankind, and the language that all of them employ to fashion themselves.

At the same time, however, even those who unmask this duplicity cannot escape it. Its most divinely sanctioned announcer, the ghost of Hamlet's father, supposed in memory by his son to be spotless at the level of God himself, or Hyperion at least (I. ii. 140), reveals himself as permeated by "foul crimes" needing to be "purged away" by other-worldly and *this*-worldly cleansings of the past (I. v. 11-12). This unexpected revelation not only gives Hamlet a reason for wondering if the ghost is a deceptive appearance (as his father now turns out to have been); it also makes him admit, in his effort to frame the fact of rhetorical man within inherited dictates, that he himself must be just as inconsistent, that the sins of the father are his own inheritance quite as much as is the duty to avenge the sins against the father/God's sovereignty and chastity. Hamlet's inability to leap the gap between true motive and visible act is now more of a problem than ever because it seems built into the divided human nature that he, as much as anyone else, incarnates. He must be one of the targets of his own satire and, while accusing others, "accuse me of such things that it were better my mother had not borne me" (III. i. 123-24).

Yet again, there is "mother" to get him out of this bind. Now gender politics enters the process of analysis as indispensible to a character's (or person's) quest for identity. If man is other than himself in his own eyes because of the ideologies he uses to form a concept of "self," he can have no definite self unless he displaces that otherness outside his "nature." Initially the existence of two sexes compounds this problem, since, for all the differences in their biological tendencies, both sexes also have a great number of things in common. A man seeking to be distinct thus has to see himself as very much like a woman and therefore just as spread across sexual natures as he is across different ideological concepts of being. Even so, woman's otherness-from-herself contains a key difference compared to man's: she can be a mother and bring forth another being from within and out of herself. She is more obviously other than herself in *being* herself and consequently threatens man's attempt to be a unity by contrast when he finds himself too much like her to escape his own otherness.[15] The only solution to this problem for man, as he draws to himself the right to prescribe meanings and properties to all that is outside him (hence the myth of Man naming the creatures), is to cast off from his own cacophonous being all seemingly heterogeneous feelings and possibilities. As Simone de Beauvoir long ago suggested, he sends them over into the otherness of woman where they supposedly become "her nature" and not properly "his."[16] In this way, woman's meaning becomes even more heterogeneous than it is already, sometimes in ways that leave her domesticated and powerless (too other-than-herself to own property or control her own life), sometimes in ways that grant her centralized power only under certain conditions (such as being the Handmaiden to the Lord), and sometimes in ways that allow her the power of the marginalized trickster figure, reminding us of the primal multiplicity from which "man" would escape by consigning it all, in gender labels, to "her" being.

Hamlet deals with his identity crisis by taking this very course, and the consequences for women in the play are precisely those just outlined. To be sure, the Prince has a problem using the power plays that language allows him. He wants assumptions about gender so codified that he can say "conceit in weakest bodies strongest works," just as the ghost says (III. iv. 115), without being questioned by anyone, including women. But he soon discovers that he cannot install self-division into women exclusively without running up against his connection with what he would make "hers." If, for example, he can make Ophelia both obedient virgin and deceiving whore in the same speeches, becoming both scourge and fool in urging her to "get to a nunnery" as both convent and brothel, he can do so only because her incoherence is like his ("We are arrant knaves all," he tells her at III. i. 128-29), only because she might become a "breeder of sinners" such as himself (III. i. 122), and only in an accusatory mirror-response to her accurate indictment of him (III. i. 93-102) for giving the appearance of desire and then claiming no knowledge of his love-tokens, the very "mak[ing of] wantonness your ignorance" for which he castigates *her* (III. i. 145-146).

Nevertheless, the hegemonic cultural codes at a man's beck and call give Hamlet (and Shakespeare) plenty of opportunities to feminize self-division, particularly since such codes are fabricated appearances that mask the complexities and blurred boundaries over which they want to gain power. The rhetoric of the Fall in the Bible and most commentaries on it already makes woman the primary original sinner, especially when Adam complains to an angry Lord, "The woman whom thou gavest *to be* with me, she gave me of the tree, and I did eat" (King James version, Gen. 3:13). Such an image gives a sanctified rationale to the blatant statement in Grammaticus' *Life of Amleth* that "All vows of women become void with changes in fortune" because women differ from themselves more than men do "in their continual longing for something new."[17] Moreover, the greater potential for "conceit" assigned to apparently weaker bodies allows woman to seem more guilty of all meanings of that word: run-away fancy, self-deceiving self-worship, linguistic deception, satiric irony, and distance between appearance and motive (*all* Hamlet's propensities). Then, too, Ophelia herself, when "sane," accepts the patriarchal order and dictates of her culture so completely that she attempts to be all the things her father, brother, lover, and King load upon her, ranging from a "chaste treasure" in "danger of desire" (I. iii. 31 and 35) to a decoy temptress (really a pawn in the games of power organized by men). All these sanctions license Hamlet to shuffle his admitted inconsistency and hesitating weakness off onto woman as the primal source, the first "breeder," and the continuous embodiment of all those qualities. He starts that process as early as he can, knowing he will need "her" as a locus for what his "too too sullied flesh" will betoken about him once he confronts his nature (I. ii. 129). Woman is not simply frail, as man is; "Frailty" is given the "name" of "woman" (I. ii. 146) as though all weakness were in that gender and not in the other, in fact as if all the "falling-off [in humanity] was there" so that it could be less noticeable somewhere else (I. v. 47).

The Prince sees his mother, of course, as deserving the largest share in this relocation, and it is amazing how many sorts of lost mastery he regains from this transference. First, this scapegoating naturally absolves both Hamlet and men in general from any primal responsibility they might bear for man's self-divided "crawling between earth and heaven" (III. i. 128). In his castigation of Ophelia, he is a sinner *because* his mother bore him, because it is women only who "make [them]selves [a] face" other than the "one [which the male] God hath given" (III. i. 143-44). If fathers, whose seed is prior to women, bear any share in the sin, it is because of "What monsters [women] make of them" (III. i. 139-40). By these lights women, regarded as angelic *or* satanic (or as both, the duplicity that man finds in himself),[18] can be sidelined from the position of origin to become ancillary assists or blocks in the passage of purity and unadulterated power from male parent to male child. On the one hand, if a woman is "good," as in Hamlet's first soliloquy on his mother, she is so only as a cannibalistic parasite. She "hangs on" her male lord, somewhat in the manner of Adam's rib, and increases her "appetite" by "feeding" on the man she worships, all the while granting him the god-like position of having the power to protect her from "the winds of heaven" (I. ii. 141-45). On the other hand, the same woman becomes a whorish Duessa when her "lust" turns away from the "radiant angel" toward an unsanctioned alternative whom she allows to deceive her in a "shape of heaven" (I. v. 54-55). Either way, whether as a conduit—and part, really, of the patriarch's body—or as a being arrant and separate from man, a criminal bringing sin into the world, woman serves man's law by acting as its obedient channel or by seeking her value away from that center in a man who himself seeks to *be* that center. In either state, she is both subservient to and clearly removed from the center of power.

Woman in this logic is an object for man's manipulation in just the fashion that gives him the most authority in the world. She fawns on him and passes on his seed or his will, or if she refuses with her own will, she is the focus of his self-exalting judgment. Her secondariness is now so complete, despite the remaining presence of all her qualities in men, that she need not be physically punished; indeed, if she were, she would not be available to serve as a beautiful excuse for contests of power exclusively among men (King Hamlet vs. Claudius or Prince Hamlet vs. Laertes). Were she so abused, moreover, her role as scapegoat would not be sufficiently disguised for man (and thus Hamlet) to be raised above her contamination as the judge of her sin. Stating this judgment directly to his mother using strong words and not real daggers, in fact, is what finally allows Hamlet to regain some confidence in his ability to translate motive into action (III. ii. 381).[19] The ghost may intervene to turn Hamlet from a harsh castigator into a more gentle and advisory confessor, thus preventing the Prince's stance from protesting too much and revealing how forced and fabricated such a power play really is (III. iv. 113-16). But that redirection mainly allows Hamlet to keep his

aristocratic pose as enactor of the ancestral command while shunting
the quandary of rhetorical man into the lap of his mother with his
urging that she "Assume a virtue, if [she] have it not" (III. iv. 161).
Woman more and more becomes the symbolic means by which the
hero's ideological conflict can be divided and conquered in his own
eyes *and* by which the original sin that should have resolved it earlier
can be both taken out of man and subjected to the control of the
Father's Son or priest.

Still, this rhetorical-political performance does not license a
man at once to fulfill motive in action (apparently) by taking arms
against male rivals. What all this can ultimately mean for woman-
kind must first be fully demonstrated and staged if man is to stage
himself by contrast as the actor able to overcome the disorders that
would "perhaps trouble a woman." The demonstration, of course, is
Ophelia's mad scene, played out in a dialogue with Gertrude (in the
only woman-to-woman confrontation in the play) while Hamlet is
off the stage effecting further changes in his rhetorical stance. Here
the younger woman's "madness," a result of male dominance and
castigation, offers a strikingly sane critique of this blatant imposition
on women in general. Now acting as both the dirty-mouthed
strumpet and the innocent, empty-headed babbler that all the men in
the play have tried so mightily to make her, Ophelia sees "the
beauteous majesty of Denmark" offering "love" to women as really
an overweening campaign for phallic power symbolized "By his
cockle hat and staff" (IV. v. 21-25). She also exposes the virgin/
whore construct as forcing women to be both at once, to be
conquered by being divided, particularly in her song of a "maid"
addressing "Saint Valentine" in which the girl becomes the holy
man's novice by losing her maidenhood to him (IV. v. 48-55).
Ophelia's parting shot is thus an unequivocal replacing of responsibility: "Young men will do't if they come to't. / By Cock, *they* are to
blame" (IV. v. 59-60, my emphasis). Precisely by thoroughly
becoming the anomaly men have asked her to be, she announces a
mixture of styles, a breaching of distinctions, a multiplicity of being,
a unsurpation of power, and a conflict between ideologies—all that
men fail to acknowledge in themselves—in verbalizing this play of
differences back to men (and sanctioned women) from the position
of the mad scapegoat crying forth from the wilderness. *She* now plays
the fool unmasking court rhetoric (including Hamlet's), relieving the
Prince of a role whose duplicity he could not escape and so revealing

clearly what he has ceded—and the *fact* that *he* has ceded it—to her gender.

But Shakespeare, as Stephen Greenblatt points out, uses each staged "challenge to [his] culture's every tenet" primarily so that "hostile improvisation" can be made safe for the dominant "ideology" trying to mediate conflict—can be positioned, while revealing itself, to support "the power of the prince who stands as an actor upon a stage before the eyes of the nation" and "the power of God who enacts His will [the ground of the Prince's] in the Theater of the World."[20] The revelations in Ophelia's chants are immediately suppressed by being called "mad," are interpreted as resulting from the loss of a male center or guide, and are sacrificed or exiled to dissolve into mobile nature while the culture seeking to control nature tries to remain unaffected.[21] Before Ophelia even appears in the mad scene, a "Gentleman" (perhaps in order to remain securely a gentleman) describes the significance of her "speech" as "nothing," a "botch" of "words" (IV. v. 7 and 10). The King then attributes all she says to the death of her father (IV. v. 75-76), and Gertrude, after the maid's drowning, pictures her (almost in a mirror image of the Queen herself clinging to her old place under the antiquated sovereignty of the patriarch) as wound in "garlands" of "dead men's fingers" and pulled down to a "muddy death" where she can sing scandals no longer (IV. vii. 167-82). Those who attend to her, all these speakers agree, are "hearers" like those among the now-restless "rabble" who unintelligently forget "custom," misunderstand the true "props of every word," and might dare "treason" against the "divinity that doth hedge a king" in aristocratic thought (IV. v. 9, 102, 104, 105, and 123-24).

Ophelia's rebellion, if acknowledged as such, threatens total revolution much in the way the misdirected will of the people does, and those people are called "false Danish dogs" even by Gertrude in their willingness to act "as [if] the world were now but to begin" entirely anew (IV. v. 1, 10 and 103). The maiden's madness must therefore be employed to redirect the Laertes whom the people have placed at their head. He, as Ophelia's brother seeing his earlier dictates internalized by her, yet mixed in a way that violates *his* patterning of them, must be led to read her as a "document in madness" fashioned so by one other young aristocrat in particular (IV. v. 177) and not by the King or any other official authority figure, even though that view of the matter is one of the biggest lies in the play. The otherness-from-themselves that she and the "distracted multitude" represent, the people being once as devoted to Hamlet as they presently are to Laertes (IV. iii. 4-7), can now become a point of dispute over which young male aristocrats can fight in the hope of controlling it, thereby keeping power in the hands of God's chosen "noble men." They are the guardians of self-division now instead of its principal exemplars, especially as they recognize, manage, cast out, avenge, and bury its insanity, sequestering it from and within themselves most of all. Assured of the madness, drowning, and imminent burial of Ophelia and all she embodies, Laertes, like Hamlet, can momentarily weep till "The woman be out" of him (along with revolution) and then be ready to act in the interest of his father's memory—and the King's suggestions—without the womanish "folly that drowns it" getting in the way (IV. vii. 187-90).

Here, starting in Hamlet's male *alter ego* when the Prince himself is off the stage, lies an explanation of his greater resignation and self-assurance when he returns to Denmark in Act V. The self-division made largely, but fictively, female has loudly declared the unfairness in its creation, the rebellion in its marginality, and the way its anomalous nature questions, even satirizes, the dominant order of words and ranks. Nonetheless, it can at last drown under long-established male pressure and be buried in a secret, unsanctified way (V. i. 213-25). At that point it can become a non-threatening memory, the now beneficent scapegoat,[22] to be recalled as a "fair" weakness deserving a man's mournful compassion (he *is* mourning parts of himself) and insisting on his watchful, indeed self-aggrandizing, command over its interment (V. i. 227 and 230). Death suppresses the threat that woman might reveal how she has been misconstructed for the sake of male supremacy; "let her paint an inch thick," Hamlet says to Yorick's skull, repeating one of his earlier methods for making Ophelia more self-divided than a man, "to this favor she must come. Make her laugh at that" and not at gender exploitation (V. i. 181-83). This neutralizing of a challenge *by* death helps redefine the hidden mystery *in* death that has heretofore aroused Hamlet's fears about having to face that "undiscovered country." Now death, by shrouding it all in impenetrable mystery, becomes the reassuring image covering and thereby suppressing the ideological conflict, the use of scapegoats to diffuse that conflict, and the fact that the cacophony ascribed to women remains the nonidentical basis of Hamlet's identity. If there is a self-division from himself or an irony in man, it has been made to seem the death that now absorbs the women and fools who might point to a different foundation. Man's insufficiency becomes his being doomed to die while striving to be more divine than he is. It is the curse that came with Original Sin, a distancing between the Father and his sons, which, by removing women from the powerful role of mediator between the Lord and His male children, reestablishes the quest for identity as seeking to mend the broken line between Heavenly Sire and fallen, mortal man. In comparison to what the struggling Hamlet has hitherto felt, he must feel relieved that he can finally interpret the problem of identity as no more than his death-bound inability to match his own will to the will of the ultimate Father.

Finally, after gaining some confidence in his ability to act from a power play against women which he now hides under the cover of death as constructed by the concept of the Fall, Hamlet has a conflict-free basis on which to enact the initial dictates of Heaven and a nicely repressive ground on which he can meet death with the assurance that he will die a hero unconnected with the "gainsgiving" that might make him seem feminine. With all events and people now betokening for Hamlet the distance or fall from, and yet the connection to, "a special providence" (V. ii. 208-09),[23] he concludes that "There's a divinity that shapes our ends,/ Rough-hew them how we will" in our fallen sense of them (V. ii. 10-11), and so he resigns himself to whatever opportunities for action (such as duels with Laertes) come his way. He believes that in them he will carry through his truest Father's hidden motives, that in meeting all challenges without probing the womanish deceptions in them he will seem entirely the male heir worthy of the Father, and that in gladly facing inevitable death in the person of a male rival he will meet the ultimate conqueror of woman *as* male power (armed even with a sword) and entirely on his Heavenly Father's terms, be death "now" or "to come" (V. ii. 210). Once the Prince accepts this "readiness" for whatever the highest Patriarch (the locus of true identity) decides to let fall (V. ii. 211), a divine retribution or poetic justice is quickly meted out to all the sinful courtiers in a way that no earthly man or woman has planned. In the end Hamlet *is* legitimately the "scourge and minister" of Heaven that feminine "gainsgiving" would have kept him from being.

To be sure, woman in this final scene does assert once more her

ability to be the marplot of male supremacy. Out of the control of
Hamlet, Claudius, Laertes, and all the gentlemen of the court,
Gertrude drinks from the poisoned cup intended by her husband for
her son, showing all plans laid by male aristocrats to be capable of
easy miscarriage and reversal. Even so, the Heavenly Father, the male
playwright, and the hero-son repossess and manipulate this aberration so as to bring about the long-awaited completion of a divinely
sanctioned quest for male power. As Gertrude expires, the long-
deferred injunction from On High to kill Claudius the usurper, to
restore the rightful male succession, is performed by the Prince on
the grounds of a "Treachery" that is manifest mainly in the
poisoning of the Queen (V. ii. 298-301 and 308-09). In case there
are any lingering signs of ideological conflict after the graveyard
scene, Hamlet resolves them by using Gertrude to help him play
"rhetorical man"—to justify his killing of Claudius in the eyes of his
immediate courtly audience (who begin to shout "Treason" until
they hear that Gertrude's poison was "tempered by" the King at V.
ii. 317)—while also fulfilling his great ancestor's demand to execute
Claudius and "leave" Gertrude "to heaven" (I. v. 82-88). In
addition, the reconstitution of free-willed woman as victim before an
audience becomes the "seed" allowing man to assume the power of
originating action. Hamlet at last becomes "pregnant of his cause" by
subsuming woman's power to bring forth from within as woman dies
away.

    This moment epitomizes the gender politics on which all the
major turns in Hamlet depend. The cup betokening and concealing
male deception and self-division is drunk in by woman so that she
embodies it all even when man is explicitly to blame. That
scapegoating allows man to stand over against this "poison," to
make it what he can interpret, cast away, circumscribe, avenge, or
turn into a tool of Providence. Moreover, that appropriation is made
right at the instant, indeed because of the instance, in which woman
exercises a will of her own outside male plans. After this transference
is completed, the polluted figure becomes the outlaw object (or at
least a symbol of the law's violation) compared to which the
ideological oppositions in male thinking can seem unified, especially
if the parts of that conflict are supposedly located or rooted in her.
Such an object, now unable to have legal power without male
assistance, thus becomes something men can fight over to decide
how it (or she) can be dealt with under the legalized purview of some

male power. Meanwhile, woman, who could and sometimes does announce the *real* maneuvers setting up this power, is kept from speaking in any sanctioned way by the later stages of the process, preferably in her disappearance behind the cloak of death. Certainly that is the muffled position that woman occupies by the end of this play that has relied so much upon her. Hamlet's demise seen as a sacrificial honoring of his father and mother will allow him to reappear in Horatio's stories about him as only the noble unraveller of masculine "purposes mistook" (V. ii. 373). The Prince's command in his dying words is not to be disobeyed. Aside from what a male defender and eulogist is permitted to tell the public, aside from what details will allow Hamlet to be borne "like a soldier to the stage" even though he has never been one (V. ii. 385), "the rest"—the relation of all crafted male "identities" to the oppressive construction of woman—must be "silence" (V. ii. 347).

III

Such an approach to reading and teaching "classics" brings me to my second proposal. For this kind of analysis will certainly seem strange or forced to students unless the whole notion of literature is redefined for them. At present in college literature classes, even when we look at the historical background that such writing transforms (refusing to see a text as the composition *of* an historical perspective serving the ideological or counterideological ends of its time), we still generally uphold the René Wellek /Austin Warren definition of what is "literary" so well circulated in their *Theory of Literature* from the late 1940s right through the 1970s.[24] In this view, truly "literary" works, as opposed to scientific or journalistic writings, are those which "tighten" and reorganize "the resources of everyday language" so as to jog us into an aesthetic "awareness and attention" that is apolitical, "disinterested," and suggestive of new and richer thought-and-sound connections that have yet to be approached in "ordinary discourses" attached to more provincial cultural interests.[25] Such a definition is profoundly bourgeois. It places a high value on the unique and free individual's capacity to reorganize perceived complexities in a way that fashions a new product, apparently transcending the ideologies of different classes, out of ingredients to which everyone supposedly has equal access.

Above all, this idea assumes that a writer's basic material, language, is composed of widely agreed upon meanings for words. Words refer to what Wellek and Warren call "norms" or "standards," conventions which most readers of the author's culture can interpret easily, despite the possible slippage of many phrases across different meanings for them. All words, we are told, "exist in [a clear] collective ideology, changing with it" rather than putting its cohesiveness in question. A "disinterested" abstracted interplay is possible in a text because there is a unified form of ideology that transcends and subsumes more local belief systems. It is remarkable—though hardly surprising, given the bourgeois foundations of academic life—how this neutralizing (and neutering) view of cultural production has maintained its dominance in the American university even in the face of, in fact by incorporating, rival theories from psychoanalysis, archetypal anthropology, phenomenology, structuralism, and deconstruction.[26]

And yet few other definitions of literature can be so easily questioned to the point of revealing a foundation other than the stated one, a foundation that demands another kind of definition. We are tempted to ask why Wellek and Warren never substantiate the existence of a "collective ideology." We find that *Theory of Literature* simply accepts the expanding unity of ideas and forms that was "culture" for Matthew Arnold and T.S. Eliot and so avoids facing the actual arena of contending beliefs, definitions, and vocabularies exposed by Marx, Nietzsche, Mikhail Bakhtin, Michel Foucault, and many others, including a host of feminist theorists from Beauvoir onward.[27] Hence, we discover, what the Wellek/ Warren notion of text and ideology really advocates, without ever saying so, is the repression or marginalization of all symbolic patterns that might undercut the power of a dominant, though widely inclusive, attitude trying to limit the number of possible functions attached to problematic words (such as "man" and "woman"). The highly "interested" and political nature of this endeavor is exposed for what it is by the foregoing reading of *Hamlet*. There we see this kind of power play as the very one fabricating legalized usurpations and character identities in suppressions of ideological conflict that also try to suppress and silence the politics of gender. It should come as no shock, then, that gender politics (alongside other politics) are cast away from the Wellek and Warren definition of literature. At the same time, though, as in *Hamlet*, this ejection shows how important those politics are to literature and the culture that literature helps to create or reveal. The Wellek/Warren "literary effort"—Hamlet's effort—to fashion a "context" making the conflicting uses of words "compatible" reveals words (such as "frailty") being wrenched toward set functions by the imposition of one sex's view—and one ideological view—upon other alternatives.

Literature clearly begins with crosscurrents of attempted dominations and resistances already formed in language (indeed as *part* of the language). The resulting centrifugal dance of terms across different cultural functions in different ideological contexts runs up against the desire for a more fixed, centripetal, cultural dictionary in the quests for containment among social groups, authors, characters, or classes of speakers seeking some dominance in the production of a text. To be analyzed more accurately than it has been, literature must be resituated as the realm of this struggle and so redefined as a composition that mediates or exposes the ideological crosscurrents in a society's discourse. According to this view, literary speakers or characters work to verbalize their "natures" at some intersection of the currents where their cultural roles can be organized, or broken down, or both, usually in a combination of well-explored and as yet untapped potentials of language. Such is my second proposal— though I would not want to present it as too simply my own hope for a new "collective ideology" about literature. "Literature" is a class-based, institutionalized, relatively recent term (alien in its current sense to how a Shakespeare would have classified writings) used for bounding off certain texts for certain kinds of study or marking them for exchange roles in the economy, always in tenuous frames that will and should be altered. I would therefore make any redefinition of it not more than a provisional one for the immediate purpose of attracting student interpretations to aspects of texts too rarely considered up to now.

In any case, the textualized "individual" in this sense of the literary project is a multilevelled, vaguely bounded, many-faceted "forelanguage," to use a term proposed by Hélène Cixous.[28] He or she is a confusing interplay of felt but mysterious memories and sensations (signs in an interplay of signs already) in the process of forming connections with socially provided words or schematizations that both compound the complexity of the sign-relations and try to arrange the recollections and unfocussed desires into interpretable patterns. Hamlet frequently sees his self-division as a sheer "fighting" of emotions "That would not let me sleep" or a vague feeling of "how ill all's here about my heart" (V. ii. 4-5 and 201-02). In addition, as he "reads" this body-language, he immediately negotiates among analogues for it in his culture's discourse, as we have seen. The more the public symbolic order tries to organize the forelanguage, the more the person feels a need to stage himself/ herself with and within the symbolic structures that work to deploy the emergent being into preexisting categories. Concurrently, though, the initially tangled interaction between forelanguage and discourse resists clearly framed deployments of relations that would forbid some interconnections from being formed or acted out. Because of this openness to many possible contexts, the half-articulated drives can lead to a conflict between ideological readings of them. Multidirectional desire now has to confront social discourse as a network of power plays, as a set of restrictions on what would like to be unrestricted, and as an arena of contention between different strategies for circumscribing the forelanguage, each of them trying to contain it in a particular fashion for the sake of some organizational or economic purpose rivaling other purposes in other schemes of interpretation.

The emerging "self" is therefore caught between two primal linguistic movements: the centrifugal urge towards multiple, ever-expanding, heterogeneous relations between signs *and* the centripetal pressure of ideological language-formations that force the self to stage the urge in their restrictive areas, despite the extent to which the areas conflict with one another. Literature is the "field of play" where these tendencies encounter one another. It ranges across the middle ground on a continuum of stagings which places, at one extreme, ritualized myth or reportage and, at the other, the incoherent babble of forelanguage simultaneously trying and *not* trying to become language. Ritual, once it reaches the strictly institutionalized stage of being a rigidified ceremony or an official type of narrative, tries to confine the shaping of being to one ideological frame strictly repeated,[29] while the opposite possibility is unshaped being desiring yet resisting frames of public configuration. Literature, as *Hamlet* shows, writes through what happens or could happen when each extreme is pulled some distance toward the other without either completely reaching its opposite. The balance or imbalance between the pulls varies from work to work, but stylizing and revealing the struggle at that crux is the principal service that literature performs for society.

Once the crux becomes manifest to a reader or student, it is the tension between gender and uncircumscribed sexuality that turns out to be the most difficult tug-of-war in the entire symbolic field, the one that reveals the most ironic paradoxes in the oscillation between ritual and the forelanguage. Despite its great power, there is no way that the enforcement of gender can occur with complete success. We can easily see that the gender system employs a clearly divided set of paradigms and that these strive to attain total ritualistic control in the hope of rescuing sexuality from the indiscriminate forelanguage of erotogenic zones and networks of feeling which men and women share, albeit in slightly different degrees and locations.[30] The system's will to power first separates parts of the forelanguage into diametric differences that become as opposed to each other as the genders are, with each gender being assigned roughly half the differences. Meanwhile, this process borrows qualities of social interaction ("aggressive," "submissive") from ideologies of behavior that have tried to establish definite divisions of labor in the social order. These traits are then divided up to be joined to the supposed physical differences under each gender-paradigm, even as men work to gain control of the marketplace by consigning only certain limited areas of it to "weaker" women. At the same time, though, gender-divisions also attempt to symbolize *natural* physical tendencies which are not as neatly divided among the sexes. Gender claims to bring the clarity of sharp contrasts to a confusion of bodily sensations where the deepest biological distinctions are supposedly waiting to be revealed. Yet gender, in the end, by making the language of polymorphous sensation the test of its objectivity, has to run up against its own difference from the intersexual drives it supposedly uncovers.

Literature exists to stage, expose, and examine the many ironies that result from this basic one. First of all, writers, speakers, and characters, at least in most texts, must confront how cultural constructions of their identities cannot fully order or encompass the errant interactions between their thoughts, feelings, and word associations. These ever-expanding interplays forge ways around the confining public frames which they admittedly need for their self-definition, undermining the achievement of binary difference which the frames try so hard to produce. Hamlet fancies he has rescued himself from polymorphous sexuality by consigning that multiplicity to "woman" and banishing her altogether from the opposite level that determines social absolutes, the supposed domain of "man." "She" thus comes to embody the irrational forelanguage and is therefore established as the gender not identical with itself/herself. But this fabric begins to unravel, for such a construct of "woman" possesses qualities that might be "masculine" as well as "feminine," meaning that "woman" has broken up the symmetry and clear division that gender paradigms pursue. "Man" turns out to be partly his opposite at the heart of himself as well, unable to be named entirely by "male," especially as "what troubles a woman" shivers through the intermixed fibre of his being. Literature nearly always shows us how the socially sanctioned, publically symbolic, gendered "other" that supposedly grants us our "nature," our self-image in the world, is but a mirror of our otherness-from-ourselves within ourselves.

Meanwhile, to complicate matters further, the ritual category, "gender" itself, especially in texts, proves almost as polymorphic as what it would restrict. Much in the way sexuality in the forelanguage is a diffuse complex of bodily feelings and vague inclinations toward other beings (not just towards the heterosexual act), so gender is a categorizing operation that scatters itself across many ideologies and class formations, finding itself transfigured each time into at least slightly different formations under pressure from each different context.[31] A play between different potential forms is built as much into gender as into any verbal construct, and that transportability belies the ritualistic claims of gender fixity, diffusing and adulterating its thrust. Literature, in turn, cannot escape from such paradoxes, since it is humankind's staging ground for testing out ways in which any ritualized concept of identity can be resisted or served by shifts of signs among the different concepts. Consequently, literature is the only fabrication that can play out gender's many ways of sliding beyond, though also back toward, its usual frames. Here a dramatized person can be made, whatever his or her aims, to face the pressure of gender as it is joined and deflected by other public pressures.

Hamlet and his fellow male aristocrats thus cannot create a univocal "femininity" despite the momentary political victory in their ascription of "frailty" to "woman." When the Prince would insure the transference of his heterogeneity to women by being their dictatorial castigator, he must perform different roles with Gertrude and Ophelia even though he wants to impose the same gendered power play on each. He must be High Priest, the Chief Scourge and Confessor, to the Queen, a woman viewed within the frame of high aristocratic standing. Concurrently, though, he must act before Ophelia the strangely hybrid part of forlorn courtly lover, city magistrate, parish priest, lower class satirist or fool, and country stud (the latter in his "Lady, shall I lie in your lap?" and "O, the hobby-horse [of the morris dances] is forgot!" at III. iii. 108 and 129). This shift between class roles reflects Ophelia's: she is the daughter of a courtly figure, yet middle class enough to be "out of [the Prince's] star" (II. ii. 141). She is constituted as a sign pulled back and forth across moral possibilities, especially by Hamlet, because all the men who so describe her are forced to perceive her as an intersection of many social stratifications. They ascribe heterogeneity to her partly because she is a female scapegoat but also because she is socially different from herself in ways the Queen can never be—despite the fact that Gertrude is the adulteress that Ophelia is enjoined from becoming and never is.

Once literature manifests these sorts of tangles, moreover, it must point, directly or indirectly, at how much such male impositions on women reveal man's lack of control the more he asserts control, how his way of making the other gender secondary to his own makes "her" the locus of what is most primary in his being. Male power is supposed to be complete in *Hamlet* when primordial otherness-from-the-self is consigned to "woman" and thereby made "less" than "man's" illusion of unadulterated masculinity (the desire of the "son" to reestablish contact with the "Father"). But the casting of the forelanguage onto a scapegoat makes the scapegoat articulate a rebellious heterogeneity—the "madness" of Ophelia— that keeps slipping beyond the frame of mere woman to become the cacophonous interplay of different class-based ideologies out of which even the male hero has had to form himself. Man turns out to be governed against his conscious will, and his power is consequently put in question, by the social cacophony of possible selves harbored by "woman" because man has imposed it on her along with his forelanguage. Woman so constituted, then devalued to hide the fact, is clearly, as Cixous has argued, the "unconscious" of the "man" who gains his identity from this transference and suppression.[32] She lies behind and within all his thinking and gendered uses of language as several drives all at once: the diffuse body-language he would (but cannot) deny in himself, the reverse mirror-figure against whom he must fashion his "nature" (which she keeps forcing him to alter), and the complex of partly conflicting concepts of identity which man—and certainly Hamlet— *is* the moment he attempts to articulate himself in the social world.

In sum, literature should be redefined as the interplay between verbalized patterns of human identity where "woman" is revealed to be "man's" unconscious, the drive toward and the concealment of his fearful quest for identity across the symbolic options he must negotiate.[33] Literature must invariably place "her" at the very heart of the construct "man," in the very network of the being who could cast "her" out so that "he" might seem to "be himself" at last. This occurs even when, as in Shakespeare, the work of "literature" visibly endeavors to stay within a governing frame structured to insure several forms of male supremacy. Once woman in literature is assigned to her "otherness" by being decentered, she as the unconscious of many playful dimensions can show us, first her unfair suppression, and then the frame-breaking means by which men and women can be—and sometimes *are* being—gradually freed from rigid gender constraints. Surely, if we can show that the articulation of "improper" resistance to hegemonies is one of those symbolic acts most "proper" to literary texts, students will see the best efforts in the feminist enterprise as a basic part, though often a forgotten part, of the subject and the object of literary study.

IV

I acknowledge, of course, that in urging my proposals I am open to criticism from feminists themselves on a number of grounds often mentioned in feminist critiques of some literary theories. I have perhaps, since I am a man, used some feminist positions, as other men have done in the past, possibly to render such views harmless by putting them to the service of illuminating "classics," thereby preserving the importance of canonical texts and trying to increase my scholarly male stature with a new reading of *Hamlet*. Worse yet, in focusing on the gender politics of male-authored and male-centered texts, I have seen woman's experience in literature as an extension, reflection, and imposition of male logic. It would seem that I have denied the uniqueness of feminine being as much as Shakespeare or Hamlet appear to have done themselves. Under a challenge from feminism, one might say, I am making the literature class safe for the study of *men* by bringing some reading practices of women under my male purview in order to explain, even justify, the power of the male hero. In this process I may be too much like Shakespeare as I have construed him; I may be acknowledging gender oppression only to uphold the necessity, maybe *sad* necessity, of the traditional exaltation men gain from such acts of scapegoating. Moreover, even when I am not describing the means to male dominance, I am speaking of a "forelanguage" that could be taken as making men and women androgynous at bottom. "Androgyny" for some feminists has been a ruse proposing a unisexual level that really disguises the quest for a monolithic (male) essence, making "wo-man" its lesser extension. And on top of all this, there is that already noted concern that I have "politicized" the study of literature, perhaps to become the political guardian of "woman's life in literature" and so to duplicate an age-old method of gaining male supremacy in the face of resistance to it.

I want to close by pleading both not guilty and guilty to such charges. The reasons why I am not guilty can be rather simply stated. I have chosen to focus in this instance on a canonical male text, first because, more than most others, its gender politics have long been protected from scrutiny (at least until recently), and then because such a text, once exposed, reveals at its heart what Catharine MacKinnon rightly calls the "theme" of the "feminist perspective": "the male pursuit of control over women's sexuality," with men seen "not as individuals nor as biological beings, but as a gender group characterized by maleness as socially constructed."[34] I can find no better proof of this age-old truth than in a text of the "great tradition" written by a virtually canonized man. If this discovery means that women must be approached as refracted through a "male logic" (a gendered construct), that is because there have been, until now, almost no "femininities" outside of gender-divided and male-dominated ways of fashioning them. Classic texts enact and help us detail the steps and motives that have brought about this condition in centuries of Western life. There has never been a unique "feminine" *or* "masculine" experience unaffected by politically created symbolizations that have misconstructed both for the sake of deploying them under systems giving power to certain males, most of the time at least. I bring in the "forelanguage" too often consigned to women alone because that mobility is what has been most often misconstrued to set up absolute dichotomies permitting an "essential" and an "other" type. Such an "unconscious" so defined does not say that all human beings are simply androgynous at heart. It says that men and women are neither identities unto themselves nor entirely different from each other nor exactly the same in every basic way. Potentially their relationship is an ever-oscillating interplay of some similarities, some differences, and a change in the proportions of each from one moment to the next. Canonical literature opens this prospect to us as the alternative to traditional gender-politics, because this kind of text (when not a ritual in disguise) clearly shows dichotomizing power-grabs at work in the face of a highly playful, figurative use of language that belies the ability of any dichotomy to remain always in command over body language, cultural language, and the interrelations of ideologies that language articulates and works out. The feminist movement—and students of literature— need to realize how much such writing potentially supports women's liberation even when it most forcefully resists it.

On other counts, though, I do plead guilty, but with the proviso that I am trying to insure the kind of future cultural development that will achieve what the most visionary and articulate feminists rightly want.[35] Though I would certainly say that virtually half of the time in a literature class should be spent on the attempts of the woman's voice to find a liberating pattern in (or beyond) the male-dominated discourse with which she must start, I do advocate considerable attention to the self-articulation and gendered imprisonment of men. For I believe that the release of women—one that *must* come—toward their myriad, but now repressed, possibilities cannot occur until a similar dispersal becomes possible for men. Women cannot be free from the confines of gender-categories, after all, until the entire ritual level of gendered distinctions, seemingly carved in stone, is broken up in the minds of most of its observers of both sexes and made fluid, made ready and willing to indulge in, even to celebrate, the constant interactions between once-separated qualities that the forelanguage and play of language have always encouraged. When that event comes, men will be just as uprooted from their gender confines as women and will find themselves happily able to pursue the "woman" as well as the "man" in themselves. Canonical literature about men, read with a careful eye, shows this possibility as a real potential, indeed shows *how* it can *be* a potential. However identified and politically effective he feels after trying to cast it out of his body, Hamlet must know that the "gainsgiving," the unconscious of both sexes displaced onto woman, has been right in warning him that the scene he has been about to enter, a scene that pivots on the total silencing of woman's voice, is one that will lead him back into the male-dominated world of rivalry, polarization, and eventual death for the sake of sanctioned male power. The gainsgiving intimates another way of thinking that would not allow language or behavior to fall into such a neatly two-sided pattern, one that would avoid the final scene's forgetting of the commonalities among people and the consequent destruction of rival factions at each other's hands. As the play of Hamlet's "foolish" language and Ophelia's mad scene suggests, that other way is the discourse of part-sameness/part-difference between terms and people, leading each speaker to see his otherness-from-himself as more real and in need of other people than any of the absolutes over which polarized men strive to kill each other.

If a student can be drawn toward seeing this dimension even in male supremacy by the reading even of royalist literature, then I also plead guilty to making my revised procedure and definitions highly "political." The argument that literary art is aesthetic and disinterested is a way of avoiding the duplicities and victimizations in the class politics and gender politics which literature persistently restages in a language that comes to it permeated with "interested" drives. To see the text as an arena of contending forces, particularly the forces of ritualization and a playful resistance to it in language, is to see it more as it really is and as a suggestive recasting of an historical context which it usefully extends to us beyond its original time. It is also to see literature as the display of culture's basic potentials, of the inclination toward binary, oppressive classification on the one hand and the drive toward less confined, boundary-crossing relations among different people, words, and classes on the other.

I admit that I want my student's moral vision to be informed by an awareness of this choice, informed even to the point of making the student, man or woman, wonder about the artificiality and actual basis of gender oppositions. Should that state of mind become widespread, the "unconscious" as I describe it will already be returning from repression to save an excessively polarized world from itself, as it could not finally do in *Hamlet*. That "kingdom" should "come" so that both "women" and "men" can expand beyond gendered confines even more than they have. But it also must come, finally, to prevent the end of all human being. Left unchecked, the present climate of international polarization, with each side in myriad rivalries seeing the other as an "evil empire," will lead us surely, as such logic does in Shakespeare, toward a final blood-bath fought with weapons far more destructive than swords. The best sort of feminist vision and the best revisionary teaching of literature are two of the methods of revolutionizing thought by which this catastrophe might be prevented. If they and other methods of defusing and diffusing symbolic power do not succeed, Death will silence the unconscious as well as gender, leaving "not a rack behind." It may be that the choice literature proffers between centrifugal (interrelational) and centripetal (polarized) identities-in-language is becoming the choice between human transformation into a real, though fluid, community and the complete disappearance of all earthly life. The price of male supremacy may be "silence" indeed, and the preservation of gender is certainly not worth it.

Notes

1. Dennis Williams, Marsha Zaborsky, and Dianne H. McDonald, "Out of the Academic Ghetto," *Newsweek*, 31 October 1983: 86.

2. The best reading of this process in *Wuthering Heights* remains the one by Sandra Gilbert and Susan Gubar in *The Madwoman in the Attic: The Woman Writer and the Nineteenth-Century Literary Imagination* (New Haven: Yale Univ. Press, 1979), pp. 248-308. See also Margaret Homans, *Bearing the Word: Language and Female Experience in Nineteenth-Century Women's Writing* (Chicago; Univ. of Chicago Press, 1986), pp. 68-83.

3. *Frame Analysis: An Essay on the Organization of Experience* (Cambridge, Mass.: Harvard Univ. Press, 1974), p. 285. See also Joan Scott, "Gender: A Useful Category of Historical Analysis," *American Historical Review* 91 (1986): 1053-1075.

4. See Foucault in *The History of Sexuality, Volume I: An Introduction*, trans. Robert Hurley (New York: Pantheon, 1978), p. 93, and on the production of hegemonies, Raymond Williams in *Marxism and Literature* (London: Oxford Univ. Press, 1977), pp. 108-27.

5. Foucault's word in *Sexuality, Volume I*, p. 106.

6. I cite this play from Willard Farnham's edition in *The Complete Works* of Shakespeare, Pelican Text revised, gen. ed. Alfred Harbage (New York: Viking, 1969), pp. 933-74. Attention has been called to this issue already, I have to admit, most powerfully, by David Leverenz in "The Woman in Hamlet: an Interpersonal View," *Signs* 4 (1978): 291-308. Indeed I am indebted to Leverenz here and at certain later points. At the same time, I think he sees Shakespeare too simply as *only* critiquing an antiquated "patriarchal order" for having "cracked all the mirrors for self-confirmation" so that the woman in man cannot be seen in them (p. 308). Shakespeare is too much of a patriarchal royalist not to believe in the political necessity, as well as the lamentable effect, of such mirrors. Moreover, Leverenz goes beyond the evidence in the play when he argues that the Prince's "real struggle is to restore his mother's validation of his [gainsgiving] feelings" (p. 307). Woman clearly validates Hamlet's male identity by being the symbolic *scapegoat* he uses to displace those feelings outside himself. I do not think Leverenz pays sufficient attention to the problem in Renaissance ideologies that prompts this sort of solution. For other feminist readings of *Hamlet*, none of which go as far as the Leverenz article does, see the *Hamlet* portions of the pieces by Murray Schwartz, Madelon Gohlke, Joel Fineman, Richard Wheeler, and David Willbern in *Representing Shakespeare: New Psychoanalytic Essays*, eds. Murray M. Schwartz and Coppelia Kahn (Baltimore: The Johns Hopkins Univ. Press, 1980); Kahn, *Man's Estate: Masculine Identity in Shakespeare* (Berkeley: Univ. of California Press, 1981), pp. 21-46 and 132-40; and Peter Erickson, *Patriarchal Structures in Shakespeare's Drama* (Univ. of California Press, 1985), pp. 66-80.

7. See, for example, Nina Baym, "Melodramas of Beset Manhood: How Theories of American Fiction Exclude Women Authors," *American Quarterly* 33 (1981): 123-39; Lillian Robinson, "Treason Our Text: Feminist Challenges to the Literary Canon," *Tulsa Studies in Women Literature* 2 (1983): 83-98; Christine Froula, "When Eve Reads Milton: Undoing the Canonical Economy," *Critical Inquiry* 10 (1983): 171-78; and Susan Hardy Aiken, "Women and the Question of Canonicity," *College English* 48 (1986): 288-301.

8. The whole notion of what is "literary" is, after all, time bound, changeable, gerrymandered, and influenced by political pressures. The

definition and limits shift—and can be made by us to shift again—depending on the ideologies, gender biases, and class interests of those given the most power to set the boundaries at a particular moment (including the time of present exclusions). See Williams, *Marxism and Literature*, pp. 45-54, and Terry Eagleton, *Literary Theory: an Introduction* (Minneapolis: Univ. of Minnesota Press, 1983), pp. 1-53.

9. This revisionary critique of male-authored texts, begun systematically by Beauvoir in *The Second Sex* and extended by scholars like Kate Millett, has taken many forms during the last two decades. See, for representative examples, books as diverse as Judith Fetterly's *The Resisting Reader: A Feminist Approach to American Fiction* (Bloomington: Indiana Univ. Press, 1978) and Nancy Miller's *The Heroine's Text: Readings in the French and English Novel, 1722-1782* (New York: Columbia Univ. Press, 1980), or the revisionist readings of male-authored texts in *Writing and Sexual Difference*, a special issue of *Critical Inquiry* (8:2 [1981]).

10. Eagleton, *Literary Theory*, pp. 14-15.

11. This Marxist notion has been elaborated best in recent years by Fredric Jameson in *The Political Unconscious: Narrative as a Socially Symbolic Act* (Ithaca, N.Y.: Cornell Univ. Press, 1981), esp. pp. 103-50, and in William C. Dowling, *Jameson, Althusser, Marx: An Introduction to The Political Unconscious* (Cornell Univ. Press, 1984), pp. 76-85.

12. For a thorough, though perhaps not sufficiently sociological, description and analysis of *homo rhetoricus* in the English Renaissance and in *Hamlet*, see Richard Lanham, *The Motives of Eloquence: Literary Rhetoric in the Renaissance* (New Haven: Yale Univ. Press, 1976), pp. 1-35 and 124-43. For a sense of how much Shakespeare was conscious of the problem of bourgeois man being grounded more on future effect than on past sanction, see the recent spate of Marxist analyses of the bard, among them Paul Delany, "*King Lear* and the Decline of Feudalism," *PMLA* 92 (May 1977): 429-40; Jonathan Dollimore, *Radical Tragedy: Religion, Ideology and Power in the Drama of Shakespeare and his Contemporaries* (Chicago: Univ. of Chicago Press, 1984); Dollimore and Alan Sinfield, eds., *Political Shakespeare: New Essays in Cultural Materialism* (Manchester: Manchester Univ. Press, 1985); Eagleton, *William Shakespeare* (Oxford: Basil Blackwell, 1985); and Paul N. Siegel, *Shakespeare's English and Roman History Plays: A Marxist Approach* (London and Toronto: Associated University Presses, 1986).

13. See the explanation of the title term and the discussion of the social standing from which Shakespeare and writers like him began in Stephen Greenblatt, *Renaissance Self-Fashioning: From More to Shakespeare* (Chicago: Univ. of Chicago Press, 1980), pp. 1-9.

14. See Grammaticus' *Vita Amlethi*, part 7 ("Amleth's Revenge"), trans. William F. Hansen, in Hansen's *Saxo Grammaticus and the Life of Hamlet* (Lincoln: Univ. of Nebraska Press, 1983), pp. 106-07. The possibility of this blood-code running up against the problem of persuading an audience, however, is made potential in the *Vita* (also on p. 107) when Amleth decides he must wait to gauge public opinion before he can safely come forth and announce the murder of his uncle as fully justified by the code.

15. For striking exposures of the otherness *in* the body basic to woman's being, see Julia Kristeva, "Motherhood According to Giovanni Bellini," *Desire in Language: A Semiotic Approach to Literature and the Arts*, ed. Leon S. Roudiez, trans. Thomas Gora, Alice Jardine, and Roudiez (New York: Columbia Univ. Press, 1980), pp. 236-70, and Luce Irigaray's title essay in *This Sex Which is Not One*, trans. Catherine Porter (Ithaca, NY: Cornell Univ. Press, 1985), esp. pp. 28-33.

16. *The Second Sex*, trans. and ed. H.M. Parshley (New York: Knopf, 1952), pp. xvi-xxix. For an analysis of this process in individual personality formation, see Nancy Chodorow, "Gender, Relation, and Difference in Psychoanalytic Perspective," in *The Future of Difference*, ed. Hester Eisenstein and Alice Jardine (Boston: G.K. Hall, 1980), esp. pp. 12-16.

17. Grammaticus in Hansen, p. 117.

18. See Marilyn French's distinction between the "inlaw" and "outlaw" female principles in *Shakespeare's Division of Experience* (New York: Summit, 1981), p. 24. I find this book most useful for reading a play such as *Hamlet* when French surveys Renaissance gender divisions in her opening sections, rather than when she reads that play (except at certain moments in the *Hamlet* section on pp. 145-58). That may be because French is most concerned with the effects of a belief-system on the hero— the fact that "there is no mean between chastity . . . and depravity in women" for him (p. 148)—and not enough with his need to use women rhetorically as the solution to a crisis in identity construction. In any case, the general process establishing such dichotomies is even more fully explored in *The Second Sex*, esp. pp. 66-81.

19. To be sure, Hamlet again confronts the problem of not having yet acted out his motive when he compares his still "dull revenge" to the army of Fortinbras "daring" all "for [but] a fantasy and trick of fame" at IV. iv. 32-66—*after* he has been the priestly scourge of the Queen. But here, reversing his sense of action's distance from its impetus back at II. ii. 533-91 and III. i. 76-88, he staunchly affirms that "occasions" outside him *can* "spur" him as they never could before and that the ideological conflict in notions of identity has been successfully cloaked as a vague past mistake,

"some craven scruple/Of thinking too precisely on th' event" in the manner of a Wittenberg philosopher (IV. iv. 32-33 and 40-41). He could not say this before self-division almost fully belonged to woman in his eyes. Now, with all "femininity" consigned to "women," he is able to seem phallically comparable to an erect "army . . . of mass and charge" (iv. 42).

20. Greenblatt, *Renaissance Self-Fashioning*, p. 253.

21. For a useful account of the Woman as Nature/Man as Culture construct, see Sherry B. Ortner, "Is Female to Male as Nature is to Culture?" in *Woman, Culture, and Society*, ed. Michelle Zimbalist Rosaldo and Louise Lamphere (Stanford: Stanford Univ. Press, 1974), pp. 67-87.

22. See the use of the scapegoat as a deflection and relocation of social rivalry and violence, a consequently blessed as well as monstrous figure, in Rene Girard's *Violence and the Sacred*, trans. Patrick Gregory (Baltimore: The Johns Hopkins Univ. Press, 1977), pp. 250-73. Indeed Girard sees this mechanism and the rivalry (though not *gendered* rivalry) leading to it as vital to Shakespeare in particular. Cf. *Violence and the Sacred*, pp. 50-51 and 304-05; "The Plague in Literature and Myth," *Texas Studies in Literature and Language* 15, (1974): 833-50; "Myth and Ritual in Shakespeare: A Midsummer Night's Dream," *Textual Stretegies*, ed. Josue' Harari (Ithaca: Cornell Univ. Press, 1979), pp. 189-212; and of course, "Hamlet's Dull Revenge," *Stanford Literature Review* 1 (1984), rpt. in *Literary Theory/Renaissance Texts*, ed. Patricia Parker and David Quint (Baltimore: The Johns Hopkins Univ. Press, 1986), pp. 280-302. On Girard's avoidance of woman's place in what he observes, see Toril Moi, "The Missing Mother: The Oedipal Rivalries of Rene Girard," *Diacritics* 12, no. 2 (Summer 1982): 21-31.

23. How this view becomes the hero's eventual solution to the mystery in all aspects of his fallen surroundings is demonstrated best by Maynard Mack in "The World of Hamlet," *Tragic Themes in Western Literature*, ed. Cleanth Brooks (New Haven: Yale Univ. Press, 1955), esp. pp. 54-58.

24. René Wellek and Austin Warren, *Theory of Literature*, 3rd ed. (New York: Harcourt, 1956). See especially their chapters on "The Nature of Literature," pp. 20-28, and "The Mode of Existence of a Literary Work of Art," pp. 142-57.

25. This idea in Wellek and Warren carries on the widespread influence of I.A. Richards and his balancing of impulses or attitudes in poetic experiences that suspends the need to believe in any doctrines to which a text's words may allude. See Richards' *Principles of Literary Criticism* (New York: Harcourt, 1928), pp. 71-133, and *Practical Criticism* (Harcourt, 1929), pp. 255-74.

26. Certain efforts provide quintessential examples of how all these theoretical frameworks have been made to serve the text viewed in bourgeois fashion as interrelated contradictions removed from the social power plays in everyday discourse. For such an application of psychoanalysis, or rather *"psychopoetics,"* see Geoffrey Hartman, "A Touching Compulsion: Wordsworth and the Problem of Literary Representation," *Georgia Review* 31 (1977): 345-61; for archetypal criticism, where culture becomes a recurrent, whole pattern without class conflict, the "total dream of man," see Northrop Frye, *Anatomy of Criticism: Four Essays* (Princeton, N.J.: Princeton Univ. Press, 1957), pp. 95-127; for phenomenology as it aims at what Richards desires, a reader's reformulation of his strictly subjective "psychic capacity" so that he can "gather new experiences" into a widened hermeneutic circle, see Wolfgang Iser, *The Implied Reader*, trans. Catherine and Richard Macksey (Baltimore: The Johns Hopkins Univ. Press, 1974), pp. 274-94; for structuralism revealing the governing linguistic contradiction in a group of texts while losing sight of the power plays involved, see Tzvetan Todorov, *The Fantastic: A Structural Approach to a Literary Genre*, trans. Richard Howard (Ithaca, N.Y.: Cornell Univ. Press, 1975); and for Americanized deconstruction viewing "constitutive" versus strictly "performative" rhetoric as a purely linguistic contradiction in "all literary language" especially, see Paul de Man, "Semiology and Rhetoric," *Diacritics* 3, No.1 (Fall 1973), rpt. in *Textual Strategies*, pp. 121-40.

27. See, for feminist examples, Beauvoir, *The Second Sex*, pp. 53-60 and 528-54; Kate Millet, *Sexual Politics* (New York: Avon, 1970), pp. 36-46; Juliet Mitchell, *Woman's Estate* (New York: Pantheon, 1971), pp. 99-122; Linda Nochlin, "Why Have There Been No Great Women Artists?" in *Art and Sexual Politics*, ed. Thomas B. Hess and Elizabeth C. Baker (New York: Macmillan, 1973), pp. 1-39; Michelle Zimbalist Rosaldo, "Woman, Culture, and Society: A Theoretical Overview," in *Woman, Culture, and Society*, pp. 17-42; and Karin Stallard, Barbara Ehrenreich, and Holly Sklar, *Poverty in the American Dream: Women and Children First* (Boston: South End Press, 1983), pp. 5-63.

28. She uses this word with reference to an "economy of drives" or a "writing" across the body of woman, an otherness-from-the-self of "mobile complexity" that man (more than woman) has repressed in the "self." See "The Laugh of the Medusa," trans. Keith Cohen and Paula Cohen, *New French Feminisms*, ed. Elaine Marks and Isabelle de Courtivron (Amherst: Univ. of Massachusetts Press, 1980), p. 260. Cixous, however, is much indebted (though also a contributor) to Julia Kristeva's sense of "the semiotic" in several essays, among them "Motherhood According to Giovanni Bellini" (1975), and to Jacques Lacan's *lalangue* and *"jouissance* of the body" in his 1972-73 *Seminar* XX, particularly the parts entitled "God

and the *Jouissance* of Woman" and "A Love Letter," rpt. in *Feminine Sexuality: Jacques Lacan and the école freudienne*, ed. Juliet Mitchell and Jacqueline Rose, trans. Rose (New York: Pantheon and Norton, 1982), pp. 138-61. For a helpful discussion of this French elaboration of "woman," see Alice Jardine, *Gynesis: Configurations of Woman and Modernity* (Ithaca, N.Y.: Cornell Univ. Press, 1985).

29. Here I use the definition of ritual and ritualistic myth offered by Georges Dumezil in *The Destiny of the Warrior*, trans. Alf Hiltebeitel (Chicago: Univ. of Chicago Press, 1970), pp. 3-4. At the same time, though, I acknowledge Victor Turner's different sense of what "ritual" can be in preindustrial societies prior to "the contraction of the religious domain" into a univocal restrictiveness. Tribal rituals in this view often do what I think literature does: provide a field of play where the myriad possibilities of symbolizing (and thus furthering) desire encounter, resist, yet find modes of partial accommodation with "normatively structured social reality." In that way ritual/literature makes "form" out of the "indeterminacy" in social conflict without shutting the indeterminate interplays entirely down or out. See Turner's "African Ritual and Western Literature: Is a Comparative Symbology Possible?" in *The Literature of Fact: Selected Papers from the English Institute*, ed. Angus Fletcher (New York: Columbia Univ. Press, 1976), pp. 45-81, and *From Ritual to Theater: The Human Seriousness of Play* (New York: Performing Arts Journal Publications, 1982), esp. pp. 61-88.

30. At this point I admit I am choosing one side over others from among the different positions in recent French "feminisms" (some of which would disclaim the feminist label). I believe that Cixous rightly locates the "forelanguage" or "*jouissance* of the body" in *all* human bodies. It is thus recoverable by male as well as female awareness once both realize that "woman" has been made, and thus is, the place of this unconscious (see "The Laugh of the Medusa," pp. 254 and 257). On this point, then, I cannot credit some aspects of woman's *unique* otherness-in-herself that Irigaray trumpets throughout *This Sex Which is Not One*.

31. To understand this translatability of gender as it links itself to many different cultural frames of reference, see Bonnie Thornton Dill, "Race, Class, and Gender: Prospects for an All-inclusive Sisterhood," *Feminist Studies* 9 (Spring 1983): 131-48. To understand the "heteroglossia" of such an interplay between sociosymbolic orders, see Mikhail Bakhtin, particularly in "Discourse in the Novel," in *The Dialogic Imagination: Four Essays*, ed. Michael Holquist, trans. Holquist and Caryl Emerson (Austin: Univ. of Texas Press, 1981), esp. pp. 260-300.

32. Cixous, "The Laugh of the Medusa," pp. 256-60.

33. "Unconscious" in this definition cannot simply refer to the standard Freudian notion of "another stage" to which infantile and antisocial impulses are repressed. Nor can it mean predominantly the archetypal unconscious of Jung in which man confronts an *Anima* whose apparent wholeness, far greater than the man's, arouses both his longing for its reappearance in visible analogues and his fear of engulfment by a womb from which he has sprung to seek a separate identity. See "Aion," trans. R.F.C. Hull, in Jung's *Psyche and Symbol*, ed. Violet S. de Laszlo (Garden City, N.Y.: Doubleday, 1958), esp. pp. 9-22. Though the *Anima/Animus* distinction here supposedly exists in a person's collective unconscious *prior* to socialization and the effect of cultural gender concepts, such concepts viewing the sexes as strictly opposite halves that need "other halves" to give them characteristics they lack permeate, even generate, these opposed preconscious archetypes. Jung shows that and more when he writes that "the anima gives relationship and relatedness to man's consciousness" and "the animus gives woman's consciousness a capacity for reflection, deliberation, and self-knowledge," supposedly unfeminine characteristics ("Aion," p. 15).

34. "Feminism, Marxism, Method, and the State: An Agenda for Theory," *Signs* 8 (1982): 244.

35. I am particularly drawn, if they are combined with each other more than they are now, to the visions in Millet, *Sexual Politics*, pp. 362-63; Cixous, "The Laugh of the Medusa," pp. 260-64; and Carolyn Heilbrun, *Towards a Recognition of Androgyny* (New York: Knopf, 1973), especially since Heilbrun defines the desireable future as "a condition under which the characteristics of the sexes, and the human impulses expressed by men and women, are not rigidly assigned" and a "full range of experience [is] open to individuals who may, as women, be aggressive, as men, tender" (p. X). I am also attracted to the future held out by the principal speaker in "Women in the Beehive: A Seminar with Jacques Derrida," trans. James Adner, *Subjects/Objects* 4 (1984): 5-19. Here Derrida offers the prospect of a sexual difference defined entirely away from "opposition": "Opposition is two; opposition is man/woman. Difference, on the other hand, can be an infinite number of sexes," a multiplicity of avenues for many-faceted "sexuality" that are not denied or restricted to a single gender (p. 14).

SUSAN HARDY AIKEN, KAREN ANDERSON,
MYRA DINNERSTEIN, JUDY NOLTE LENSINK,
PATRICIA MacCORQUODALE

7. Changing Our Minds: The Problematics of Curriculum Integration

The preceding essays speak eloquently of the successes of curriculum integration. Their authors, through the quality of their intellectual efforts and the depth of their commitment, discovered in feminist scholarship a basis for a profound reconceptualization of their disciplinary tenets, their course structures and content, their research agendas, and the academic and cultural institutions that shape and are shaped by these constructs. As we had hoped, feminist paradigms enabled these scholars and others like them to understand what had previously seemed like anomalous data, reinterpret traditional texts, and expand the canons in their fields to include materials whose significance had earlier eluded them. In the best sense they became our colleagues and comrades, enhancing our knowledge and understanding of the feminist project as they developed their own.

The legacy of our project, however, was contradictory. While it furthered curricular reform in many important ways, it also revealed to us the magnitude and intractability of resistance to genuine feminist transformation of the academy. In order for curriculum transformation projects to be most effective, their directors need to be forewarned of the potential pitfalls they are likely to encounter. In this essay, therefore, we present an overview of the positive changes effected by our project, some speculations about the conditions that helped bring them about, and a more detailed analysis of the most significant sources and implications of the resistances we encoun-

134

tered. Finally, we conclude with questions raised by our analysis regarding the role of curriculum projects in promoting feminist change in an institution whose basic premises remain androcentric.[1]

Success Stories

At the outset, we want to affirm our sense that curriculum integration is crucial to feminist efforts to transform the academy.[2] That conviction derives in part from the fact that our project has had a positive impact in a number of areas: pedagogical, scholarly, administrative, and personal. Even when the changes were less dramatic than those exemplified in these essays, our evaluations showed that many participants made measurable alterations in the perspective and content of their courses, changes that will likely be extended and elaborated in years to come.[3] The student evaluations indicate that the project was successful on two accounts: 1) courses targeted for change included more material on women in assigned readings, syllabus topics, lectures by instructors, and class discussions; and 2) generally, students reacted positively to these materials, becoming more aware of women's issues and wanting similar courses to contain similar materials. As one participant put it, the systematic study of gender "turned on the lights for some of these kids." Another found that using gender as a central theme in the study of literature "aroused very strong discussion and sometimes very strong responses to the new women authors that I included in the course."

One of the unexpected results of the project was its positive effect on a number of graduate students working with project members. As one professor noted, "The idea of modifying undergraduate attitudes and awareness through the introductory survey courses plants one kind of potential seed that may grow and mature and reach open, broader visions. But also important are these other responses—from the women in the graduate programs—so enthusiastic and so immediate. They're the ones who . . . will carry this into their own roles as teaching assistants, especially if they're leading discussion groups." He continued: "In the case of two or three of these graduate students" at both the Master's and the Ph.D. level, "this whole topic of women and looking at women in other cultures . . .is a very exciting and profound part of their learning experience in the last year. Through the seminars, through independent study projects, and through talks with [Women's Studies faculty he had recommended to them], they became more aware of what studies of women could offer them." This professor began "a collaboration with a graduate student on the relationship of women to women as depicted in folk songs that [the professor] collected thirty years ago in India" and to which "virtually no attention has been paid in most of the literature on India and mythological literature." As a result, the student wrote a paper that was accepted for presentation at a major conference the following year.

Many who had initiated changes in their courses have continued that process as they read further in feminist scholarship and gain confidence in its methodologies. "I suppose the greatest impact" of the project, remarked one participant, "was to lead me to read a body of literature that I simply didn't know much about." "It has," said another, "changed my thinking about things basically." Often, participants have come to see material on women as vital to all courses and have added materials on women to their other, nontargeted classes as well. Indeed, in some cases, as one participant remarked, work in the project "has an almost greater effect on a nontargeted course . . . than on the targeted one" since in upper-division courses one is less affected by existing departmental requirements of the sort that often pertain in introductory surveys. As another observed, "The notion of mainstreaming as applied to students is important . . . but I think it works in reverse—on the teacher too: that it gets into his or her mainstream of ideas, which then color other courses."

In these cases, participants came to realize new implications in the term *integration*. As one professor explained, "rather than . . . simply devoting one or two lectures a semester to so-called women's issues, it's allowed me to deal with the gender issue in lots of basic lectures on general subjects, so it's not . . . been removed to a 'woman's day' or a 'woman's week' series in my class . . . ." Without the help of the seminar discussions, he continued, "I might've approached it" less holistically: "I'd have read a book on a specific woman's issue in recent [scholarship in his field] and so perhaps have given a lecture . . . . Instead what I tried to do is take issues of general significance and show the gender aspects of them, which I think philosophically, was one of the goals of the idea of mainstreaming Women's Studies . . . . It certainly worked for me that way, so that instead of isolating the subject matter, I feel that I've integrated it into a general course approach."

Indirect reports have affirmed that many participants have altered not only the content of their courses but the style in which they interact with students, especially women students, both in and out of the classroom. As one participant admitted, "I guess I found myself to be much more sexist and chauvinistic than [I had] first believed." Another reported that after becoming sensitized to gender issues, he "found a list of fellowships and financial assistance available to women . . . . [and] had that xeroxed and distributed to all women students in the department. I probably wouldn't have done that the year before." One of the women in the project noted that she had become "much more of an advocate for the women graduate students than I was before. My office was the place where the women would come and complain if something happened. But now I seek them out and say okay, if you are going to make it through this, this is what you have to do . . . . I feel much more radical about making sure that the system works for them too." A recently selected department head commented that "I've thought of ways in which I might try to get to women graduate students to talk to them about their participation in the department."

Women's Studies faculty have also reported that their colleagues who were in the project are now more sympathetic to graduate students' research on women, often referring them to experts in the area rather than—as has been too often the case— guiding them away from topics involving gender research. As one professor explained, "One of the . . . major impacts [of the project] is that I am one of the supervisors on a doctoral dissertation of a woman who is looking at women in management. I would not have considered being a part of this project or interested in it prior to the [curriculum] seminars. Now I am actively involved in doing some research on the area of this questionnaire study, trying to get at the difference in male and female. The impact has been considerable."

Participating faculty have gained new perspectives on their own research as well. As one participant put it, the project "will have far more profound effects in the future than it did [the] year" he actually participated in the seminars, for what he has experienced is "the reorientation of all of my work." Some faculty have worked to revise their current research to include more about women or have returned to materials gathered in previous projects for which they have become able to develop appropriate analytical frameworks. One remarked that "with this intellectual stimulation I got during the seminars . . . , which I found very valuable, I've gone back and launched two or three different research projects using materials I already had but had not used." Others who participated in the curriculum integration project are adopting new directions in their work, deciding, at least in some cases, that feminist scholarship represents the "cutting edge" in their fields. One commented that he was much better grounded in feminist critical theory and "it's crept into many parts of my own research which began prior to any kind of feminist training that I had. I think it's contributed a significant amount to a book I'm trying to finish now." A number of participants have presented papers at professional meetings or are working on articles and books that reflect their new research focus.

Far beyond the scope of the original plan, the project has also succeeded in changing administrative policy at the University of Arizona. Faculty who later moved into key administrative positions were impressed by the high caliber of the feminist scholarship they discovered through their participation in the project. One department head, who later became a dean, remarked that the project "was clearly well thought out and very sympathetic to the males entering the program. I felt I was working together with them rather than opposed to or against them . . . ." He also reported that he "was pleased with the level at which the discussions took place." This influence has resulted in the hiring of feminist faculty members in several departments and in positive promotion and tenure decisions for feminist scholars in others. Additionally, several of the Steering Committee faculty have been asked to serve on important policy committees. In the final analysis, changes like these may turn out to be the most far-reaching of all.

It is difficult to analyze thoroughly why some participants changed more than others, but those who took the purposes of the project seriously did share certain attributes. Not surprisingly, the most enthusiastic and successful participants were those who, for a variety of professional and personal reasons, had already developed an interest in Women's Studies. The experiences of one professor typified this pattern: "I had been doing research and teaching in this area for four or five years so it wasn't a brand new area for me. If anything, what it has done is further reinforce areas of interest here." This person is representative in another way as well: the most receptive participants often included those who already were very active in research and publication. In addition, successful participants were often more theoretically oriented than others and thus better able to recognize the epistemological necessity of working across disciplinary boundaries and to appreciate the fact that questions of gender inflect the very grounding of every disciplinary discourse. Finally, the personal was certainly the political: the most successful participants were often those who live happily with strong, independent, professional women—even more particularly, feminists—or men who have bright daughters whose aspirations their fathers share. One participant stated that support for curriculum integration could be explained "because so many of ... our wives are professional women, and really believe strongly in women's rights. Another larger percentage have teenaged daughters. . . and don't want them to become traditional women."

Looking back over four years, our assessment is that the project affected approximately half of the participants positively. Perhaps one-quarter experienced serious intellectual and/or personal changes which have dramatically altered their teaching, research, and politics. Another quarter met project goals by incorporating varying amounts of material on women and gender into their courses. The remaining half were relatively unchanged, for reasons which will be discussed below.

The Problem of Resistance

While the project made significant headway in modifying the liberal arts curriculum on our campus, it also served to reveal in stark detail the nature and depth of opposition to feminist scholarship. Situating large numbers of relatively older, generally powerful men vis-a-vis a few relatively younger, less privileged feminist women (the majority of them untenured), the project reflected in microcosmic form the structure of the university itself. Each seminar, then, became a theater wherein the gender politics of the academy operated in particularly dramatic and revealing ways.[4]

We have been ambivalent about addressing the problem of resistance: we are aware of its political implications, its potential to be misinterpreted and misused by those hostile to curriculum integration. However, while the successes of curriculum integration have been widely documented, very little has been said about the problems such projects may confront. The following analysis seeks to map that underexplored terrain. As a result of our experiences, we believe that no simple revisions of the structure or content of curriculum integration projects will suffice to eliminate the problem of resistance, but certain strategies can work to moderate its effects to some extent. By detailing the kinds of problems curriculum project leaders might anticipate, we hope to contribute to the development of such strategies. In attempting to disentangle some of the most significant sources and implications of resistances, we move from a consideration of their relatively simpler, more superficial manifestations to our theories about some of their more complex and profound sources and motivations.

At the simplest level, our hopes for what the project would accomplish were sometimes incompatible with what we could realistically expect, given the diversity of participants' goals and motivations. While a number of participants, as we have suggested, came to the project highly motivated and open to change, others came for a variety of different reasons. For a few, the grant stipend appeared to be the primary motivation. Others joined out of curiosity, intending to assess *whether*—rather than how—scholarship on women was valid or useful. Some of these seemed to decide in the negative, and sat out the remainder of the seminars, neither contradicting nor contributing. Other participants engaged in selective reading and hearing, deflecting discussions onto tangents—debating, for example, whether Aristotle or Plato better exemplified the classical tradition, or the exact beginning date of the (male) Renaissance. A variant of this mode occurred when some participants attacked subtly-argued articles as diverse (and often opposed) as, for instance, Sherry Ortner's "Is Female to Male as Nature is to Culture?" and Carole MacCormack's "Nature, Culture and Gender: A Critique," as being monolithic repetitions of the same thesis.[5] In addition to suggesting cursory reading on the part of these partici-- pants, this confusion also exhibited the degree to which stereotypical expectations about feminist scholarship could obscure the understanding of otherwise intelligent academics.

More numerous—and more frustrating—were those who, in the seminar, politely agreed with the readings but limited the changes in their thinking and course designs to an absolute minimum. In certain cases, this resistance appeared related to an unwillingness or inability to perceive the implications of feminist critiques. For example, we had chosen an interdisciplinary format not only to provide a theoretical stimulus for participants' reconceptualizations of their own disciplines, but also because the interdisciplinary approach is fundamental to feminist epistemology, which calls into question traditional academic boundary systems. Thus, participants faced a dual task: to rethink the role of gender within their disciplines *and* to interrogate the very structures on which their disciplines were erected. This group, however, had difficulty getting beyond the epistemological constraints of their own fields and theorizing across disciplinary boundaries. Such participants often found the readings irrelevant because not discipline specific. One professor, for instance, could not see a connection between our texts on women and society and his efforts to develop statistical information on the gender gap in politics through the use of public opinion polls and the like.

Some participants resisted theoretical readings in general, requesting instead primarily preassembled "how-to" classroom materials that they might fit into their otherwise unchanged courses. In some ways, this form of resistance is the easiest to understand. Given the human tendency to inertia, it is only realistic to recognize that many of us are most comfortable teaching what we already know, according to methodologies, theories, and frameworks with which we are familiar. In the absence of the motivation that comes from being a member of a disadvantaged group, people will often not exert themselves unduly to alter what they consider to be "tried and true"—in several senses of the phrase. Professors in this group usually objected that including materials on women in their courses would entail the sacrifice of something more important, rather than recognizing the necessity of precisely the sort of radical reformulation that would obviate such objections. Often, this form of resistance was revealed in rhetoric: one participant spoke repeatedly, for example, of how he planned to "shoehorn" a few women's issues into his otherwise untouched syllabus. In view of the time constraints he cited as an excuse for such limited changes, this metaphor suggested that for the women thus included, such "shoehorning" would inevitably also necessitate the academic equivalent of *footbinding*. Significantly, this preoccupation with "what to cut," like the other forms of resistance sketched above, illustrates that without genuine commitment to the legitimacy of feminist scholarship and serious consideration of its epistemological implications, academics will probably achieve only the most minimal changes. These difficulties, however, represent only the superficial symptoms of deeper, more complicated forms of resistance. It is to these that we now turn.

The Problem Of Translation

Throughout the seminars, many participants found discourses on gender both alien and profoundly troubling. We tended to underestimate the extent to which our own years of work on these issues had given us an encoded, almost shorthand system of linguistic reference with which we were at ease, but which these participants could neither translate nor speak. It became a challenge, then, to find a level of discourse simultaneously accessible to those unfamiliar with feminist thinking, and sophisticated enough to do justice to the subject. Introducing participants to feminist paradigms was not enough. We spent a great deal of time explaining basic concepts, defining essential terms, and correcting misperceptions born of partial understanding. Yet in subsequent sessions the same misconceptions and definitional questions sometimes recurred as though never addressed before. As in many teaching situations, we found it necessary to repeat distinctions and definitions many times. One participant, for instance, after six weeks in the project during which *sex* and *gender* had been repeatedly distinguished, inquired as to their difference; several other participants, near the end of one set of seminars in which the term *patriarchy* was frequently discussed, appeared unfamiliar with the word. What makes such situations different from other kinds of teaching, however, is that in addition to asking participants to learn to speak and understand feminist discourse, we were also asking them to unlearn an enormous amount of the discourse of traditional culture.

The cross-disciplinary scope of our project sometimes created other linguistic difficulties as well. A major problem with any interdisciplinary study in an academy divided along disciplinary boundary lines is that those who venture outside their own areas of specialization will often be regarded with suspicion: at best as neophytes—stereotypical tourists who cannot speak the language of the field they presume to examine and who overlook nuances and complexities apparent to the natives; at worst as dangerous trespassers, or colonizers seeking to expropriate territory not their own. Thus, for example, in a seminar devoted to exploring the underlying similarities of the perceptions of women articulated in Genesis 2-3, Aristotle's *On the Generation of Animals*, selections from Thomas Aquinas, and the *Malleus Maleficarum*, we were accused by a historian of being "ahistorical": there is, he claimed, "no common tradition" or "connection" among these texts—an assertion that overlooks Thomas's extensive use, in *Summa Theologica*, of both Genesis and the *Generation*, and the reliance of the authors of the *Malleus* on the medieval patristic misogyny culminating in the *Summa*.[6] When reminded of these intertextualities, he could not see them as germane.

This perception of territorial invasion is doubly complicated by the issue of gender. As Carole Pateman has shown, women traditionally have been perceived by masculinist thinkers as figures of what Rousseau terms "disorder," potential disrupters of masculine boundary systems of all sorts, and all the more fearsome because situated within the very heart of "civilization."[7] Given the gender ratio of our groups, this paradigm, though unacknowledged, appeared operative on a number of occasions. Under these circumstances, the participants' appeal to disciplinary boundaries seemed to serve as a rod for simultaneously measuring our shortcomings and "correcting" us, keeping us in line or in place by, as it were, disciplining us.

What these questions of linguistic competence mask is that within the academy the language of "scholarship" is inseparable from the language of power. In the contested terrain where gender is signified, the question of who owns the discourse becomes inseparable from questions of ownership of all sorts.[8] Hence, it is perhaps not surprising that when we articulated our ideas most forcefully, some participants reacted as if we had unfairly wrested control of academic debate. Confusion at this perceived "usurpation" was intensified by the fact that it was not easy to dismiss us on intellectual grounds: as scholars, we were respectable according to traditional criteria; yet they saw us using precisely the same tools of scholarly discourse that compelled their admiration, to undermine the very tradition that had developed and valorized those tools. Other participants—presenting us with a far more difficult situation—tried to contest our scholarly authority altogether, labelling our assertions as "ideologically motivated" while leaving the ideological grounding of their own epistemologies unexplored. Thus we found it continually necessary to expose the ideologies inherent in "neutral" scholarship, while also indicating that recognizing them does not inevitably leave scholars with only a mindless relativism which disregards evidence and logic.

Text And Subtext

These reenactments of well-worn cultural gender scripts were related to another form of resistance. Having volunteered to study women, many participants found that they were also forced to think about themselves in disquieting new ways. Because the feminist insistence on the social construction of gender inequality constitutes an implicit (and sometimes explicit) critique of men, it challenges masculine self-images and involves many men in a curious dilemma. If they assume both their own agency in social processes and the injustice of women's secondary status, then they must acknowledge complicity in gender imbalance. Curriculum transformation projects ask that they commit themselves not just to lip-service to such attempts but to genuinely radical reconceptualizations that would put in question their inherited bodies of knowledge and some of their most cherished assumptions, procedures, and methodologies. Yet such commitment means relinquishing their positions as self-defined custodians and beneficiaries of a "meritocracy." On the other hand, refusal or failure to initiate changes creates guilt and dissonance between their actions and their self-images as just and thoughtful people. To maintain their self-respect, they had to reconcile such dissonances. For those participants who saw themselves as liberal and sympathetic toward women, yet who resisted the thoroughgoing transformation implicit in the feminist project, the implications of this conundrum were all the more stinging.

The emotionally-fraught nature of this situation was revealed at a number of levels. Whenever discussions deal with sexuality— especially in the context of a feminist awareness of sexual politics— they are probably bound to provoke highly-charged emotional responses, particularly, perhaps, from those people who think that they have transcended or are liberated about such things. The provocative and potentially threatening nature of the material made it inevitable that the seminars functioned simultaneously on at least two levels: an intellectual, consciously "rational" discourse was set in tension with dynamics approaching those of an encounter group. That is, the meetings had both an explicit text and a potentially explosive subtext, a kind of communal "unconscious" often unrecognized or unacknowledged by the participants (and—at least at the outset—by us) but all the more potent for such repression. Not surprisingly, this situation sometimes produced very negative dynamics, absorbing much time and energy.[9]

Anxieties within the seminar were further exacerbated by the inversionary gender dynamics of the group, in which women occupied the unsettling position of experts. Some participants seemed to experience this positioning as a direct threat to their authority, to feel—even though the program was voluntary—that we constituted a kind of "police force" (or, as one of them insisted on characterizing it, a group of "schoolteachers"—that stereotypical spectre of every schoolboy's nightmares: "unfeminine," "frigid," wielding the phallic ruler with emasculating force). While attesting to the power of the ideas we sponsored, this defensiveness was a block to their acceptance.

Our experiences make it clear that the tools of rationality alone are inadequate to the task of intellectual change when the investments in ideas about gender are so deep-seated and self-interested for all parties. We had consciously chosen to use primarily a conventional ratiocinative approach, concerned lest systematic recourse to the experiential or affective would alienate participants and reinforce stereotypes about both female academics and feminist studies as "emotional" and "unscholarly." In addition, we wished to maintain a collegial relationship with our participants beyond the project itself. It is evident to us now, however, that a tension between text and subtext invariably arose and that there is no obvious or easy resolution to this dilemma. In no other area of the project did the disparities between academic profession/practice and the gendered double standards they create cause more difficulty. Even when discussions operated on a very abstract level, we were often accused of "talking about ourselves" in a particularistic, subjective, and self-interested way. On the other hand, participants often advanced their own particularisms and subjectivities as universal, neutral, truth-seeking rationality. Unless feminist scholars can successfully expose and deal with the subterranean emotional text of this discourse, our academic legitimacy will remain suspect. Yet to do so is, ironically, to risk reconfirming the stereotypical prejudices that have for so long prevented us from being taken seriously within an academy which requires "objectivity" and rewards those whose claims to detachment are most widely acknowledged by their peers.

The Nature Of Things

Although challenges and vigorous debate can promote substantive discussions around central intellectual issues, they can also prevent, minimize, or deflect the consideration of the major premise of feminist scholarship: the sociocultural construction of gender. Denying that crucial premise, some participants were forced to fall back on rationalizations based on easily-accessible pieces of our cultural baggage—biological determinism, human capital theory, functionalism, and the like. Participants' readiness to resort to such constructs reveals their continuing strength even among liberal academics and reminds us to take seriously the conventional belief structures which we might otherwise dismiss.

The frequency of recourse to biological interpretations of gender asymmetries, in particular, took us by surprise and posed a real challenge to a serious consideration of cultural interpretations. The extent to which the influence of sociobiology and other biological perspectives pervades the academy became clear as participants from across a wide disciplinary range alluded to the premises of these fields, although their familiarity with the actual literature was not necessarily extensive. Some discussants relied on hormonal sex differences to explain human gender asymmetry, while others focused on "Man the Hunter" as the progenitor of contemporary male dominance. In several cases, ideas centering on women's putative inferiority in intellect and assertiveness were favored as explanations for cultural inequality.

These discussions of biology and gender difference often raised with particular acuteness the question of scholarly neutrality and detachment. References to activities of other animal species as paradigms for human behavior—a common form of intellectual shorthand, if not shortcoming—often characterized the discussions. One participant, for example, cited the treatment of mares by stallions as proof of the "naturalness" of traditional gender divisions of power. The "man-as-hunter" argument was vividly exemplified by another participant's claim that males "of all species" are hunters, proving that men "naturally" have higher achievement motivation. Challenged by a participant who specializes in physical anthropology, he ignored her evidence and accused her of "misrepresenting scientific facts."

On another occasion, during a scheduled session on objectivity, one participant stated that the major problem with feminist research was that it rejected the possibility of the biological inferiority of women. Whereas other fields of inquiry would admit any kind of answer, he said, feminism discounted a priori one major area of research and its interpretive possibilities. (However, when we suggested that he substitute race for gender in this paradigm, the implication of his remarks became evident.) Some proponents of the idea of women's intellectual inferiority tried to distance themselves from this position with disclaimers that they were viewing the possibility only as hypothetical. In this context another professor suggested that one can clarify such issues with students by taking the position that even if women are inferior, that does not justify enslaving or oppressing them. Such an interpretation allows the men who hold it to retain their sense of superiority, to protect their power and privileges, and to secure their self-images as fair and caring people even while making claims on women's gratitude. Under this construction, rights for women devolve into compassionate policies for the defective. As these examples make clear, the frequent imprecision and misinformation of appeals to "Nature" suggest not only lack of knowledge but another—possibly unintentional—agenda: such appeals at once convey and veil the defense of male prerogative historically inextricable from arguments about women's "natural" inferiority.

In response to these biological arguments, in the second year of the project we introduced readings on biology and gender asymmetry and on male resistance to feminist change. These strategies yielded mixed results. When, for example, we used Ashton Barfield's "Biological Influences on Sex Differences in Behavior," a lengthy, scrupulous summary of the major research on the biological bases for sex difference, many participants complained that we had devoted too much attention to the issue.[10] Nevertheless, possibly due to the difficulty of refuting Barfield, this group did not charge us with misreading biology for political reasons. On the other hand, when we chose to focus explicitly on the political nature of all such materials through using articles by E.O. Wilson, Stephen Jay Gould, and Ruth Hubbard, one participant attacked Hubbard, a Harvard biologist whose feminist critique of sexism in science he perceived as an attack on science itself. Because Hubbard contested the idea of absolute scientific objectivity, often regarded (especially by non-scientists) as a foundation for scientific inquiry, her work was characterized as dangerous and thoughtless. It is worth noting, however, that Gould, who agreed with Hubbard, did not evoke the same hostility.[11]

Ultimately, whatever strategy we adopted toward biological determinism met with some resistance, suggesting the intractability of the issue. Those participants less interested in discussions of biology worried that we devoted far too much time to it. For others, however, biology was *the* central issue; our insistence on devoting systematic attention to the social construction of gender left us—and feminist theory—open to charges of political bias. Given the import of this issue for gender scholarship, we propose that biological considerations should be formally included early in curriculum integration projects. Although formal discussion did not enable us to move beyond biology with complete consistency, it did reduce the likelihood that consideration of other topics would be sidetracked.

On the other hand, our attempt to deal with male resistance by introducing materials that explicitly analyzed it seemed to elicit profound levels of hostility, for which feminist criticism became the object: seen as the contagion, as it were, that engendered male dis-ease. A discussion of William Goode's sociological analysis of "Why Men Resist," for example, became a model of unacknowledged resistance, epitomizing the dynamics participants sought to deny and allowing some participants to distance themselves from any complicity.[12] To refute Goode's claim that men benefit from traditional sexual arrangements, some participants pointed to the liabilities men experience under present arrangements (such as higher heart attack rates) or to the advantages they might gain for supporting feminist changes (such as more "leisure" time to spend at home). These arguments implicitly minimized both women's oppression and men's role in its retention, displacing the problems of prejudice and discrimination to different times, places, or social groups. As one professor put it, prejudicial attitudes might exist in the general society but not among academics "if they are people for whom ideas matter."

Even when the readings contained only an implicit and indirect critique of men, many participants became uncomfortable. In the seminar that included major Western thinkers from Aristotle to Rousseau, for instance, our choice of readings came under attack as biased, designed simply to make men look bad. A survey of traditional thinking on gender does indeed expose most authors who ordinarily qualify as academia's heroes and masters to be variously unreflective, derivative, or myopic on the subject of women. Parallels in these traditional works to contemporary masculinist perspectives exacerbate the resistance. In our workshops, some participants' desire to retain their identification with the tradition while avoiding an *open* endorsement of its gender scripts led to tortured constructions of the texts or to a denial of their centrality in the Western tradition. Their sexism was defined as tangential and anomalous or was interpreted out of existence. For example, several professors dismissed Aristotle's pronouncements on gender in such texts as *The Generation of Animals* and the *Poetics* as "peripheral" and "insignificant," not realizing or not admitting their implications for the conceptual foundations of his philosophy. Another scholar interpreted the myth of the Fall in Genesis 2-3 as an indication that Adam had got the worst of things: *he* was cursed to endless toil while women were "only" burdened with increased fertility, pain in childbirth, and subjection to men.

The Persistence Of Difference

The conviction that women had little particular or legitimate basis for grievance, past or present, surfaced frequently. Some participants used discussions of other inequalities as the means to discount the importance of gender. They also suggested that because a few groups of women had held certain forms of power over some men, women in general experienced few problems in gaining access to power and privilege. Indeed, that women had occasionally exercised authority over socially disadvantaged males even became the unacknowledged measure of how profoundly these men had been oppressed.

Several participants used the relative oppression argument, comparing (white) women's status with that of black and poor men (not black or poor women), as a means to label all women's concerns trivial. In these discussions, other unintended revelations occurred. One participant remarked that it bothered him in discussing inequality that "we talk about this and then attribute it to the problems of women when to a large extent it can be attributed to the problems of young people or . . . the problems of talentless people or people without access or whatever it might be." (In view of the fact that the Women's Studies faculty in the workshop included women who were generally younger and had less institutional power than the men, this remark is instructive.) This sort of argument was pushed to its limit by a professor in another seminar who suggested, without ironic intent, that we had neglected the problems of discrimination against "the ugly."

The denial of gender points to another problem, at least as complicated: the ambiguous question of "gender blindness." Some of the participants, who often identified themselves as liberal, decided to promote "exceptional" women—often discovered in the course of the seminars—to the status of "honorary men," eliding the specificities of gender difference. Some literature professors, for example, sought to assimilate female authors into the "great tradition" of *master*works, without realizing that that tradition, and the critical categories historically used to define it, are themselves put radically into question by women's writing. The underlying assumption of this form of gender blindness, of course, is that men remain the measure of human significance and signification. Thus they can continue to speak for/as women, in effect rendering women themselves unnecessary, redundant, and mute.[13]

Admittedly, human commonalities do exceed differences— even gender differences. On some level, as John Stuart Mill long ago observed, as long as sex/gender systems operate, we simply cannot know what a gender-free "humanity" might mean.[14] Indeed, one of the major debates animating contemporary feminisms concerns the problem of at once adequately distinguishing sex/gender difference and comprehending a human being that transcends gender lines, acknowledging the internal differences within each of us that render problematic all traditional, simplistic categorizations of the "self" as necessarily "male" or "female." As Hélène Cixous has pointed out, such reductive gender oppositions are dangerous precisely because they have traditionally been used to justify those systems that would keep women in their "proper" place.[15] Yet the perils of regarding "woman" and "man" as monolithic, universally and eternally opposed categories should not obscure the equally pernicious error of assuming no difference at all, which, as Adrienne Rich observes, leads to a reification of the category "human" as equivalent to "male" and thus subsumes and erases women yet again: "The urge to leap across feminism to 'human liberation' is a tragic and dangerous mistake. It . . . recycles us back into old definitions and structures, and continues to serve the purposes of patriarchy."[16]

The ineluctable presence of difference made itself felt in another way as well. We had hoped that eventually, as a result of their work with the project, participants would come to see the human experience—"male" and "female"—through the eyes of women—to attain what Virginia Woolf calls a "difference of view."[17] Although some participants attained this viewpoint at times, and a few achieved an intense understanding of it, many sought repeatedly to return to the topic of men. Ultimately, they resisted seeing either women or themselves from women's perspectives—indeed, some appeared to disbelieve that any such perspectives existed. This focus on men could be used in a positive way to highlight the significance of gender as a factor of analysis, leading men to understand women's oppression through developing an understanding of their own. Yet such discourse can also serve as a strategy for evading identification with women, thus retaining men as the focal point of inquiry.

Even when the seminar topics and readings focused directly on women, such androcentric diversions occurred. In a discussion of a chapter on women's "emotion work" from Hochschild's *The Managed Heart*, several participants immediately shifted their attention to the imposition of emotion work on men in American society.[18] Despite the efforts of the moderator and others to bring the subject back to women, these participants repeatedly returned again to a focus on men, who (they argued), to function in a hierarchical world, are expected to sacrifice authenticity and self-esteem for the "feminine" tools of indirection and manipulation. To demonstrate lost masculine status and the tragic impossibility of male omnipotence, participants cited Lee Iacocca's troubles at Chrysler and Henry Kissinger's subordination to Richard Nixon. At one point, two discussants debated at length about housework, attending entirely to its relevance to men's lives and omitting serious consideration of the implications of the question for women themselves. This androcentric focus was particularly evident in the final presentations on the curricular transformations participants had developed. There, many talked at length about disciplinary canons and paradigms rooted in male experience and then finished with only brief discussions of women, often represented as anomalous—literally ab-normal.

Unfortunately, some participants who transcended masculinist preoccupations and attempted to voice feminist positions frequently found their contributions ignored or discounted by others in the groups, or found themselves subtly renamed "female"—read "inferior"—by some of their colleagues. Often, under these circumstances, the professors being criticized tended to disown the very insights they had articulated. One participant, for example, early in the seminar delivered a stinging feminist critique of the idea of the objectivity of knowledge, only to retreat, by the end of the term, into traditional masculinist gender paradigms. Even some of those men who changed dramatically often, perhaps necessarily, did so with a certain detachment from the insights provided by the materials. Others talked about their feminist sympathies only in private conversations with us, wary of exposure in the public arena.

What all these examples demonstrate is that men still enjoy greater freedom to select the terms of their discourse than do women. As Nancy Miller has wittily observed, "only those who have it can play with not having it."[19] But this "freedom" may be illusory: the male peer group—not to mention androcentric culture and tradition—exercises a considerable tyranny over many of its members, in effect acting as a tacit police force over their discourse, hence over thought itself.

Male domination of discourse also revealed itself in the gendered conversational patterns well documented by feminist linguistic scholars. At times even the most important topics and perspectives we introduced would only be seriously attended to when reintroduced later by a male participant. Similarly, we often heard women discussed as though none were present. When this pattern became pronounced enough that we pointed it out, the group in question did not perceive it as a significant or systematic problem. (In fact, they hadn't even noticed.)

To the extent that the most resistant participants heard us at all, however, what they generally heard were our criticisms, which they often assumed to be invalid. After one particularly heated discussion of human reproduction in which Women's Studies faculty joined with many participants to disagree with the presenter, his reaction included the conclusion that the women had been unreceptive to his point of view, their understanding of his presentation clouded by "emotionality." He failed to notice that many of his male colleagues had objected as strenuously as we. The perception that the seminar dynamics pitted women against men (each perceived to be monolithic in their views) all too frequently shaped and signified the unacknowledged subtext for the discussions.

Seeing (As) The Other

What does this mean for women? Throughout our four-year experience, we were continually reminded that phalloreferential/reverential discourse assumes many forms. We also found striking confirmation of Nancy Chodorow's observation that men have used their cultural hegemony to express and institutionalize "their unconscious defenses against repressed yet strongly experienced developmental conflicts."[20] Curriculum integration asks men to value the female, the very element they had unconsciously rejected in their formation of gender identity, and to relinquish traditional culture, the very construct with which they had identified in expressing and allaying their anxieties about separation, selfhood, and power.

As the foregoing analysis suggests, even when the desire to learn about women was sincere, the conceptual/psychological difficulties inherent in the process sometimes proved formidable. In the face of mutual misunderstanding, both men and women involved in such a project fear objectification: ultimately, each group on some level perceives the other as a threat to its autonomy and selfhood. In the highly-charged context of contemporary gender relations, all generalizations about gender group attributes and behaviors, however carefully qualified and explicated, carry the threat of such objectification. Women, however, having been historically relegated to Otherness far more pervasively than men, are especially vulnerable to this dynamic. Thus we were particularly sensitive to its enactment in a variety of ways in the seminars: the implicit and explicit derogation of women, the silencing tactics, and the trivialization of feminist scholarship designed to invalidate our perceptions and call our scholarly integrity into question. We were also attuned to the dangers of woman's erasure through what Catharine MacKinnon calls "aperspectivity": the contention that the male view is the unbiased view, that the "neutral observer" is in fact really neutral— as well as neuter.[21]

For some of the men, on the other hand, the process functioned as an unsolicited interrogation of their unexamined assumptions and practices not only as scholars but also as human beings. The primary threat of the seminars for them was that, in being objectified by us as "the Other," they would become, in every sense, "unmanned." Their attempt to "know" women entailed the fearful possibility of being *known by them*, of relinquishing the security and privilege traditionally enjoyed by man-the-knower. As Simone de Beauvoir has observed, "man dreams of an Other not only to possess her but also to be ratified by her."[22] This "dream" is profoundly disturbed by feminist scholars' refusal to accept men's premises uncritically, to ratify unquestioningly their positive self-images, or, more importantly, to play out the masculinist scenario described by Beauvoir, wherein women"consent" to their own oppression by first putting up an intelligent resistance to the idea of their inferiority and then capitulating—deferring to men's opinions of women and of themselves. As Beauvoir remarks, man requires "that this struggle remain a game for him, while for woman it involves her very destiny."[23] That the unwritten rules for this cultural "game" may no longer function is deeply unsettling.

As we seek to become our own translators, then, we must remain alert to the linguistic and conceptual pitfalls inherent in such a project and mindful of its emotional as well as its cognitive implications. As long as scholars remain rooted in the Western academic tradition of distance, detachment, and denial, retaining the conviction that scholarly "neutrality" is the necessary condition to promote objective truth-seeking, this dilemma will persist. Yet when feminists challenge the very idea of neutrality in scholarship, or question traditional conceptualizations of "the self," they are frequently, as we were, accused of "rampant relativism" and of replacing academic standards with ideological frameworks. The anxieties of participants stemming from this issue did not derive simply from a desire to evade the political implications of the materials or from a projection of their own fears regarding a loss of control and a sense of separate identity: their anxieties were inseparable from their socialization as academics. This particular form of resistance, it would seem, may well be predicated by the very structure of the institution within which, problematically, we must operate even as we seek its its transformation.

What all these examples illustrate is the dynamic at the heart not only of curriculum integration efforts but of culture itself: the problem of difference. Fundamentally, the issue is one of perspective.

Each man and woman reads our culture's gender scripts from where s/he stands. For feminist scholars, the project of changing men's minds is therefore inseparable from inducing them to change the ground—intellectual, emotional, academic—from which they assume their point of view, and in so doing to redefine "woman's place" as well. The ambiguities inherent in our curriculum project, and its potential for being read in completely opposite, mutually contradictory ways by women and men, became for us a figure for the whole cultural process, confirming time and again what we all know only too well: that the scripts that underwrite masculinist culture are well-learned and intensely resistant to change.

Changing Minds

As we remarked at the outset, we have discussed resistances to curriculum integration because we feel that only by exposing these dynamics can we develop effective strategies to deal with them. The difficulties we confronted do not diminish our belief in the importance of such projects, nor our sense of the significant successes they achieve. It is imperative to remember that change takes many forms: in addition to the rapid and dramatic conversions and the documentable modifications we witnessed, we would also stress subtler, less easily demonstrable forms of change: the slow, incremental, but nonetheless significant processes that only began with our project but will have positive, expanding effects for years to come. By keeping these continually in mind, one can simultaneously maintain high standards and expectations and avoid succumbing to discouragement when these appear unfulfilled.

Curriculum integration is, however, an exceedingly complex undertaking, as we have tried to suggest. Those who direct it should anticipate resistances that will shift in both kind and intensity according to the changing chemistry of the groups involved. Because resistance assumes such protean forms, there is no single "right way" to proceed; nevertheless, from our experience we would offer the following, by no means exhaustive, suggestions for avoiding some of the pitfalls we encountered:

In addition to the obvious needs for the project—administrative support and financial resources to provide stipends and/or released time for project directors and participants—we found that it is extremely helpful to have a strong Women's Studies Program in place before attempting curriculum integration. Such a program offers many useful resources, including a faculty experienced in working together and in maneuvering amid the ever-shifting currents of the gender politics on a given campus. The presence of such a program also emphasizes that curriculum integration is not a replacement for Women's Studies but an extension of it.

Women's Studies faculty should retain control over the project, carefully selecting the participants and dispensing the rewards so as to insure accountability for outcomes. It is important to involve as many *senior* Women's Studies scholars as possible. While we counted on the authority of the *texts*, it is only realistic to recognize that the power of the individuals presenting the material has much to do with its acceptance. We would also suggest a balance of junior and senior, tenured and untenured, participants.[24]

Similarly, the diversity of feminist theory and of women's experiences—especially relative to questions of race, class, ethnicity, and sexual preference—should be emphasized from the beginning. Not only does such a focus prevent participants from overgeneralizing about women as a group; it is essential to adequate analytic understanding of gender issues.

The interdisciplinary nature of our project necessitated a highly theoretical approach, the strengths and weaknesses of which we have noted above. Retrospectively, some of us wonder whether providing more disciplinary focus (at least in the beginning) and more immediately usable readings directed at specific courses would have worked better. In either case, project leaders should be explicit from the outset about the feminist assumptions that ground the project, and be prepared to explain and discuss these issues a number of times. They should also use caution in deciding whether to offer readings that directly analyze men's roles and behaviors, since such texts may elicit explosive reactions. Should leaders experience these defensive dynamics, we think it useful to draw attention to them as they occur.

Because burn-out is a besetting problem in the case of lengthy projects, the larger the pool of feminist scholars you have to draw on, the better. Project leaders should anticipate the enormous time commitment curriculum projects demand and be prepared to deal with their own inevitable frustrations and impatience—humorously, if possible—both in and out of sessions with participants. Above all, do not blame yourself if the changes you have worked for so arduously seem painfully slow.

Having tried (and been tried by) curriculum integration, our sense of accomplishing this difficult task is tempered by our equal skepticism about the possibilities of achieving the ideal of a transformed academy. We are left, at last, with questions. Some of these confirm the concerns expressed by Mary Childers in her incisive negative analysis of curriculum integration. We find especially compelling her sense of the danger that participation in the program may give uncommitted, even hostile professors "unofficial credentials as faculty with competence in Women's Studies"[25] and that we may unintentionally "contribute to programs" that produce "a false sense of satisfaction" with the degree of institutional change that has been accomplished (p. 166). In sponsoring the authority of those with only the shallowest conception of feminist scholarship, do we not do Women's Studies a grave disservice?

We wonder, too about the long-term effects of the curriculum project on our colleagues and our institution in the context of pragmatic local politics. We have noted that in some cases administrators impressed by the quality of feminist thinking shown by the Steering Committee faculty have supported the advancement of their careers and looked favorably on hiring feminist professors. On the other hand, we also know that the rudimentary knowledge of feminist scholarship which the project imparted to 46 faculty members is now considered by some administrators to be adequate for the entire curriculum, making unnecessary any more systematic and effective policies to ensure student exposure to materials on women. And while the feminist scholarship in the project impressed most of our colleagues, it confirmed for certain others their greatest fears about "knowing women": that Women's Studies has moved beyond a simplistic oppression model on which all liberals could agree, to a call for fundamental changes in our social arrangements and conceptualizations. Some male faculty became so deeply angered when we contested their epistemologies and their most basic perceptions of sexuality that we must now acknowledge their active enmity.

Further, our experience supports the validity of concern about the perils and paradoxes of institutionalization. As Childers rightly observes, there is a danger that "increasing emphasis on convincing our colleagues of the value of what we do may lead to a process of selection that will leave out precisely what is most radical and promising in Women's Studies" (p. 164). We wonder, as she does, whether the compromises necessary to curriculum integration may not only foster this "softening of the message of feminism" but also "mean that our own . . . feminist consciousness" may lose some of its edge (p. 165). The ultimate danger of a philosophy of compromise, as Childers suggests, is that "by revising her message to make it palatable for non-feminists in power," the "feminist speaker [may lose] something of herself" (p. 166).

There is another loss, not potential but all too real: the professional costs of this project to us. Just as some of our participants asked, "What must I leave out of my courses in order to include women?" so we must ask what we were forced to leave undone in order to conduct this four-year endeavor. Should we not, perhaps, have devoted to our own research those hundreds of hours we spent planning, conducting seminars, and assessing our project? The politics of the academy make it virtually impervious to transformation without the pressure brought to bear by feminist scholars who have attained the institutional "legitimacy" tenure and promotions confer; we still need many more senior feminist professors in influential positions both locally and nationally. Such positions, we all know, generally presuppose prolific and high-quality publication. Would not the additional time and energy we would otherwise have given to our own work perhaps ultimately have brought about greater institutional change by contributing more to the enhanced visibility and respectability of feminist scholarship within our disciplines and by increasing our own opportunities to exercise transformative influences within the profession? Is the fired, refined vision of what feminist scholarship entails that we now bring to our research worth the time we had to take away from it?

Yet ultimately we refuse the artificial and simplistic dichotomy this instance might suggest: to assume that individualistic scholarship alone can become the means whereby we establish the legitimacy and necessity of feminist transformations is to ignore our past and to disregard the institutional basis of our oppression. The exclusion of feminist frameworks from "mainstream" courses and scholarship constitutes an overt, if unacknowledged, policy of containment on the part of academics confronting feminist challenges in their disciplines, the academy, and the society at large. We must somehow strike a balance, then, between our valid need to press ahead in establishing our critical concerns as individual scholars engaged in a collective enterprise of revision while also working together within the academy to contest the androcentric premises on which it is based. Neither strategy alone is sufficient, but we must be creative and realistic in devising those means whereby each effort enhances the other.

Are the gains achieved by curriculum projects worth their psychological and emotional cost? On this point, we remain ambivalent. We found especially that we had not anticipated adequately that the suppression of anger would constitute one of the most difficult and personally costly requirements of the project. We found, moreover, that combating defensiveness and maintaining some detachment from the implicit or explicit negative reactions of some of the participants became more difficult as time passed. Though we managed, on the whole, to preserve a patient and detached demeanor, with surprisingly few lapses into impatience or defensiveness, the psychic cost of such self-control was enormous. We now wonder whether we should have expressed our anger more directly and honestly.

Perhaps the most dangerous aspect of suppressed anger is its potential for displacement. We found that living with high levels of frustration and stress over four years finally began to put a considerable strain not only on each of us individually but also on the personal relationships within our group. Because our communal unity was our ultimate defense against the hostility and derogation of the more resistant participants, even small misunderstandings among us could appear painfully magnified. These divisions, which often occurred, significantly enough, along disciplinary boundaries, usually also involved differences over feminist perspectives— especially ironic in view of some participants' belief that we adhered to a monological "party line."

There is, however, a positive side to this question of emotional cost. While stress can admittedly render one dysfunctional, we remember that the emotional grounding of our work is also one of its strengths: without the passion of generations of feminists, we who now benefit from their sacrifices would not be in the academy, or in any of the other traditional bastions of masculine privilege, at all. Moreover, our collective anger—and what one might, using Monique Wittig's alteration of a male metaphor, call the camaraderie of the trench shared by all *guérrillères*—brought us into a unity of purpose which surpassed anything we (who had been colleagues and friends long before we began the curriculum integration project) could have foreseen or imagined. Since the individualizing, competitive nature of the academy is one of the major forces that would disempower academic women, we now see this enhanced cohesiveness as one of the most important unanticipated benefits of the entire project. This crucibled melding made our group into a stronger force for change than would ever have been possible otherwise and will clearly endure far beyond the curriculum project, empowering us for future efforts to bring about feminist transformations within the university.

Notes

1. For a more complete analysis of the resistances we encountered in the project, see our article "Trying Transformations: Curriculum Integration and the Problem of Resistance" in *Signs: Journal of Women in Culture and Society* 12:2 (Winter 1987). 255-75.

2. The exclusion of feminist frameworks from "mainstream" courses and scholarship constitutes an overt, if unacknowledged, policy of containment in the face of feminist challenges to traditional disciplines, the academy, and the society at large. We believe it necessary to strike a balance between Women's Studies programs, which are essential for both intensive and extensive focus on women, and collective efforts to transform the traditional curriculum and to contest the masculinist premises on which it is based. Without that transformation, Women's Studies programs risk continued ghettoization.

3. Evaluation data were collected in the courses that were targeted for change and in a group of unchanged courses matched according to size, level and department.

4. In this essay, we focus on the male participants in the project because we hesitate to generalize about so small a sample of women. Further, because there were only three women in the project, it is impossible to insure their anonymity.

5. Sherry Ortner, "Is Female to Male as Nature is to Culture?" in *Woman, Culture, and Society*, ed. Michelle Rosaldo and Louise Lamphere (Stanford: Stanford University Press, 1974), pp. 67-87; Carole MacCormack, "Nature, Culture and Gender: A Critique," in *Nature, Culture, and Gender*, ed. Carole MacCormack and Marilyn Strathern (London: Cambridge University Press, 1980), pp. 1-24.

6. For examples of commentaries on Genesis 2: 4b-3 that relate the text to patriarchal reactions to Canaanite mother goddess mythologies, see E.A. Speiser, *Genesis: Introduction, Translation, Notes* (New York: Doubleday, 1964), and Bruce Vawter, *Genesis: A New Reading* (New York: Doubleday, 1977), esp. pp. 46, 70. See also Mary Daly, *Beyond God the Father* (1973; rpt. Boston: Beacon Press, 1974). In discussing this, the more ancient version of the two creation narratives in Genesis, our focus was on the dominant Judaeo-Christian interpretive tradition that has grown up around it during over two millennia and has persisted, with amazing tenacity, in the popular imagination and within several major religious traditions, to this day. See, for an analysis of this tradition, Bernard P. Prusak, "Woman: Seductive Siren and Source of Sin? Pseudepigraphal Myth and Christian Origins," in *Religion and Sexism: Images of Woman in the Jewish and Christian Traditions*, ed. Rosemary Radford Reuther (New York: Simon and Schuster, 1974), pp. 89-116. There are, of course, revisionist readings of Genesis 2-3—beginning with Phyllis Trible's pathbreaking "DePatriarchalizing in Biblical Interpretation," *Journal of the American Academy of Religion* 41 (1973): 30-48—in which feminist theologians and Biblical scholars have attempted to disentangle the text from this interpretive context. See also Trible, *God and the Rhetoric of Sexuality* (Philadelphia: Fortress Press, 1978). For other examples, see Phyllis Bird, "Images of Women in the Old Testament," in Reuther, ed., *Religion and Sexism*, pp. 71-77; Carol Meyers, "Gender Roles and Genesis 3:16 Revisited," in *The Word of the Lord Shall Go Forth* (ASOR: 1983), pp. 337-54; Mieke Bal, "Sexuality, Sin, and Sorrow: The Emergence of Female Character (A Reading of Genesis 1-3)," in *The Female Body in Western Culture*, ed. Susan Rubin Suleiman, pp. 317-338; and Esther Fuchs, *Sexual Politics in the Hebrew Bible* (Bloomington: Indiana University Press, forthcoming), and Carol Meyers, *Discovering Eve: Ancient Israelite Women in Context* (New York: Oxford University Press, forthcoming). While we addressed the possibilities such reinterpretations open up, we were primarily concerned to analyze precisely the hegemonic power the androcentric tradition has maintained, and the reasons for its dominance and persistence.

7. Carole Pateman, "The Disorder of Women: Women, Love, and the Sense of Justice," *Ethics* 91 (October 1980):20-34. See also Natalie Zemon Davis, "Women on Top: Symbolic Sexual Inversions and Political

Disorder in Early Modern France," in *Society and Culture in Early Modern France*, ed. Natalie Zemon Davis (Stanford: Stanford University Press, 1975), pp. 124-151. Also reprinted in *The Reversible World: Symbolic Inversion in Art and Society*, ed. Barbara A. Babcock (Ithaca: Cornell University Press, 1978).

8. We were continually reminded of the truth of the fundamental feminist insight that the intellectual tradition is and has been used to rationalize male dominance. As Adrienne Rich has eloquently put it, the university, like other social institutions, is still "male-centered," "a breeding ground not of humanism, but of masculine privilege. As women have gradually and reluctantly been admitted into the mainstream of higher education, they have been made participants in a system that prepares men to take up roles of power in a man-centered society, that asks questions and teaches 'facts' generated by a male intellectual tradition, and that both subtly and openly confirms men as the leaders and shapers of human destiny both within and outside academia." "Toward a Woman-Centered University," in *On Lies, Secrets, and Silence: Selected Prose, 1966-1978* (New York: W.W. Norton, 1979), p. 127.

9. Interestingly, this effect can go on beyond seminar bounds, establishing a genealogy of negativism from one year of a project to the next. One participant, for example, sat in virtual silence through a whole series of meetings. Unknown to us at the time, he had been concealing a great deal of anger. The following year, a much more verbal man entered the project, bringing not only his own ambivalences but the anger of his quieter colleague, who had confided in him the previous year.

10. Ashton Barfield, "Biological Influences on Sex Differences in Behavior," in *Sex Differences: Social and Biological Perspectives*, ed. Michael Teitelbaum (Garden City, N.Y.: Anchor Press, 1976), pp. 62-121.

11. E.O. Wilson, "Sex," in *On Human Nature* (Cambridge, Mass.: Harvard University Press, 1978), pp. 121-48; Stephen Jay Gould, "Biological Potential vs. Biological Determinism," *Natural History Magazine* (May 1976):12-22; Ruth Hubbard, "Have Only Men Evolved?" in *Discovering Reality*, ed. Sandra Harding and Merrill B. Hintikka (Cambridge: Schenkman, 1979), pp. 45-69.

12. William Goode, "Why Men Resist," in *Rethinking the Family*, ed. Barrie Thorne, with Marilyn Yalom (New York: Longman, 1982), pp. 131-50.

13. On men's speaking for/as women, see Elaine Showalter, "Critical Cross-dressing: Male Feminist and the Woman of the Year," *Raritan* (Autumn 1983):130-49 and Nancy K. Miller, "I's in Drag," *The Eighteenth Century: Theory and Interpretation* 22 (Winter, 1981): 47-57.

14. *The Subjection of Women*, in John Stuart Mill and Harriet Taylor Mill, *Essays on Sex Equality*, ed. Alice Rossi (Chicago: The University of Chicago Press, 1970), p. 148.

15. See "Sorties," from *La jeune nee*, trans. and rpt. in *The New French Feminisms*, ed. Elaine Marks and Isabelle de Courtivron (New York: Schocken Books, 1981), pp. 90-98.

16. Rich, *On Lies*, p. 134.

17. Virginia Woolf, "George Eliot," in *The Common Reader, First Series* (New York: Harcourt Brace, 1925), p. 176. See Mary Jacobus' astute remarks on this phrase as it relates to "the nature of women's access to . . . male-dominated culture," in "The Difference of View" in *Women Writing and Writing About Women* (New York, 1979), pp. 10-21.

18. Arlie Hochschild, *The Managed Heart* (Berkeley: University of California, 1983).

19. Nancy Miller, "The Text's Heroine: A Feminist Critic and Her Fictions," *Diacritics* 12 (1982):48-53. Miller's article occurs in a dialogue with Peggy Kamuf's "Replacing Feminist Criticism," pp. 42-47 of the same issue.

20. Nancy Chodorow, "Gender, Relation, and Difference in Psychoanalytic Perspective," in *The Future of Difference*, ed. Hester Eisenstein and Alice Jardine (Boston: G.K. Hall, 1980), pp. 3-19.

21. Catharine MacKinnon, "Feminism, Marxism, Method and the State: An Agenda for Theory," *Signs* 8 (Summer 1983):635-658.

22. Simone de Beauvoir, *The Second Sex*, trans. H.M. Parshley (New York: Alfred A. Knopf, Inc., 1970), p. 170.

23. Ibid., p. 172.

24. Though the goals of our project, as we have noted, limited our selection to tenured participants during the first three years, during the fourth year we included a broader mix of participants, allowing the participation of certain untenured professors whose achievements in the project were outstanding.

25. "Women's Studies: Sinking and Swimming in the Mainstream," *Women's Studies International Forum* 7, no. 3 (Special Issue, 1984): 163. Further references to this article appear parenthetically in the text.

Index

negative, 134-35, 140, 156-67; positive, 134, 135-39, 159-60; on pedagogy, 41-45, 59, 101; on personal lives, 50-56, 159-60; on project leaders, 156-57, 158-60; on research, 45-50, 59, 158-59
—and epistemology, xiv-xv, 59, 139,—141
—and gender identity, 153
—goals of, 78, 140, 135
—interdisciplinary focus of, 139, 156
—institutionalization of, 157-58
—problematic aspects of, 157-59
—projects, xv-xvi, xxiiin8, 39-41, 157
—resistances to, 134-35, 139-55; analysis of male, 148-49; and biological determinism, 146-48; and discourse, 142-44; and gender "blindness," 150-51; and gender differences, 149-53; and group dynamics, 145, 148, 152-53, 162n.9; and interdisciplinary focus, 141, 142-43; and male identity, 144-46, 153; and objectification, 153-54; political implications of, 139-40; and subjectivity, 145; and women's perspectives, 151-53
—responses to, xviii, 53, 98; androcentric focus in, 151-53
Curriculum, traditional: and women, xi-xv

Delinquency: gender differences in, 80; and socialization, 81
Derrida, Jacques, 17, 33, 133n.35; critique of, 36n.9
Desire: male, and woman's identity, 4, 27; female, 37n.13
Determinism, biological, 47: and political theory, 7; and resistance to curriculum integration, 146-48
Deviance, criminal: and socialization, xx; theories of (male), 86-88
"Differance" (Derrida), 17
Difference: and language, 17, 23; problems of, in curriculum integration, 149-53; and sexuality, 133n.35
Differences, Gender. See Gender Differences.
Dill, Bonnie Thorton, xxiiin8, 132n.31
Disciplines, academic: development of, xii-

xiii; reformulation of, xiv, xvi, 72, 139, 141; traditional divisions of, xv, xvi, xvii, 60-63, 64-65, 142-43, 159
Discourse: and culture, 32; on gender, and resistance to curriculum integration, 142-44; and language, 15-16, 118; masculine/patriarchal, 1-2, 23-31, 32, 33, 124, 152; and power, 118, 125; and reality, 18; women's, 6, 23, 27-29, 30, 31, 32, 38n.24. See also Language
Disorder, and women, 110, 143
Disruption, woman as, xiii
Diversity, women's, xxi-xxii, 47-48, 156
Doctor Faustus (Mann), 2
Dohm, Hedwig, 5-6
Domestic violence, relation to state, 66, 67, 73n.3
Domesticity, and masculine power, 4
Domination: and cultural containment, 117, 158; and gender roles, 99; male, 47, 109, 110, 112, 126, 152, 162n.8; masculine, and political power, 3-5; and political theory, xvii; and theoretical discourse, 2
Dumezil, Georges, 132n.29

Education for Critical Consciousness (Freire), 45
Education: and androcentrism, xii; exclusion from, xi-xii
Eliot, T.S., 116
Elites, and traditional political theory, 61
Entrapment, of women, 4
Episcopal Church, women in the, 51-52
Epistemology: of traditional political theory, 59-63; and feminist scholarship, 7-8, 82, 86, 141, 146; and gender, 86, 139; and gender differences, xvi, 85; and power, 2, 144; scientific, and positivism, 84-85; and subjectivity, xix
Equality, gender, 2, 12
Essentialism, 47, 123; in development of political theory, 11-12, 71
Ethics: of care, 89-90, 91-92, 93-94; in Hegel, 9-11; of rights, 89, 90, 91-92
Ethnicity, xxi, 48, 156
Evaluation, 160n.3; of traditional courses, xxiin6; of integrated courses, xxivn8, 135
Exclusion, women's: from political theory, 1-2; from the university, xi-xv